D0811564

Religion and Counseling

The Continuum Counseling Series

Religion and Counseling

The Psychological Impact of Religious Belief

Robert J. Lovinger

Foreword by William Van Ornum

Continuum | *New York*

1990

The Continuum Publishing Company
370 Lexington Avenue
New York, NY 10017

Copyright © 1990 by Robert J. Lovinger
Foreword Copyright © 1990 by William Van Ornum

All rights reserved. No part of this book may be reproduced, stored in a retrieval system, or transmitted, in any form or by any means, electronic, mechanical, photocopying, recording, or otherwise, without the written permission of The Continuum Publishing Company.

Printed in the United States of America

Library of Congress Cataloging-in-Publication Data

Lovinger, Robert J.
Religion and counseling : the psychological impact of religious belief / Robert J. Lovinger ; foreword by William Van Ornum.
p. cm. — (Continuum counseling series)
Includes bibliographical references.
ISBN 0-8264-0486-3
1. Psychology and religion. 2. Counseling. I. Title.
II. Series.
BF51.L68 1990
158′.3—dc20 90-32689
CIP

For David and Mark

Contents

List of Tables and Illustrations

Foreword

The Continuum Counseling Series—the first of its kind for a wide audience—presents books for everyone interested in counseling, bringing to readers practical counseling handbooks that include real-life approaches from current research. The topics deal with issues that are of concern to each of us, our families, friends, acquaintances, or colleagues at work.

General readers, parents, teachers, social workers, psychologists, school counselors, nurses and doctors, pastors, and others in helping fields too numerous to mention will welcome these guidebooks that combine the best professional learnings and common sense, written by practicing counselors with expertise in their specialty.

Increased understanding of ourselves and others is a primary goal of these books—and greater empathy is the quality that all professionals agree is essential to effective counseling. Each book offers practical suggestions on how to "talk with" others about the theme of the book, be this in an informal and spontaneous conversation or a more formal counseling session.

Professional therapists will value these books also, because each volume in The Continuum Counseling Series develops its subject in a unified way, unlike many other books that may be either too technical or, as edited collections of papers, may come across to readers as being disjointed. In recent years both the American Psychological Association and the American Psychiatric Association have endorsed books that build on the scientific traditions of each profession but are communicated in an interesting way to general readers. We hope that professors and students in fields such as psychology, social work, psychiatry, guidance and counseling, and other helping fields will find these books to be helpful companion readings for undergraduate and graduate courses.

From nonprofessional counselors to professional therapists, from students of psychology to interested lay readers, The Continuum Counseling Series endeavors to provide informative, interesting, and useful tools for everyone who cares about learning and dealing more effectively with these universal, human concerns.

Religion and Counseling

Most people in the United States have some kind of religious faith or outlook. Yet, how many therapists and other mental health workers understand the important role of religion in mental health? Unfortunately, many clinicians shy away from examining the important place of religious belief in the thoughts and feelings of their clients.

Robert Lovinger's *Religion and Counseling* offers an examination of the many ways the Christian, Jewish, and Islamic traditions are related to contemporary mental health. This is a book to help all counselors broaden their awareness of clients. Anyone interested in religious themes—and statistics indicate that most Americans have some church affiliation—will find this an informative and sometimes provocative book.

When a person talks about religion, says Lovinger, "the person is telling me useful things about his or her world, but not in plain English. I hear these themes as expressing important aspects of their past or present experience, but in a religious idiom." Many counselors and therapists believe that Freud himself was against religion and saw it as pathological. "Freud," says Lovinger, "did not hold that religion was false in The Future of an Illusion, but that it contained significant wishes."

Many times religious outlook becomes woven with life problems that counselors deal with on a daily basis, including: alcoholism, conscientious objection, mourning, depression, healing, homosexuality, extramarital affairs, annulment and divorce, and prayer. Lovinger provides case examples and dialogue to help us understand both religious beliefs and emotional concerns in these issues.

Although it is not as heated an issue as a decade ago, many people, especially parents of teens and young adults, wonder about the role and effect of cults and New Religious Movements (NRMs). Lovinger looks at the psychological needs in young people or other converts that such movements address, and he offers practical commentary on approaches such as deprogramming. The issue of "satanic cults" is addressed. "There seems to be less than meets the eye in most satanic churches and groups," Lovinger concludes.

Many practical questions and concerns are addressed throughout the book. How do the three major religions in the United States—Judaism, Christianity, and Islam—express themselves in the everyday lives of their faithful? How have different American churches evolved over the years, and how are they related to each other in beliefs? What does it mean when a client asks a counselor to pray with him/her, and how should the counselor handle this request? When a counselor works with a client of a faith unfamiliar to the counselor, can it be helpful to ask the client for information to read on that faith? How can knowledge about the Bible or about scriptural quotes and themes be helpful to the counselor in understanding the person? How can the counselor work in a collaborative manner with a person from the clergy?

Robert Lovinger brings his expertise as an experienced

therapist and he also demonstrates a wide knowledge of the literature and beliefs of many religious orientations. He is also a member of Division 36 of The American Psychological Association—Psychologists Interested in Religious Beliefs, a group of psychologists dedicated to understanding the important interactions between religion and psychology.

Religion and Counseling will help all counselors to recognize the important emotional dimensions of religion, and will also be of interest to any reader desiring to learn more about the dynamic and vital relationship between psychology and religion.

William Van Ornum, Ph.D.
Marist College
Poughkeepsie, New York

General Editor
The Continuum Counseling Series

Acknowledgements

Many people have contributed to this book. In addition to the tutorial provided by my clients in some of the many forms of religious expression, I want to acknowledge the help of Kim Belland and Ann R. Clynick with specific sections of the text. Joseph Frankenfield was always available to answer questions about the manifold aspects of Roman Catholic life and endured, with good humor, stubborn errors on my part. William Van Ornum, editor of this series, was supportive in a number of ways, including tolerating time "overruns" until the manuscript was completed. Kyle Elaine Miller at Continuum was always available and helpful with the complexities of the publishing process, while Cynthia Heller's careful proofreading measurably contributed to the clarity of the text and helped me say what I intended, sometimes in spite of myself. To all of them I am grateful. Special gratitude and appreciation is due to my wife Sophie for timely reading of problematic sections of the manuscript, her inability to understand what was not clear and her emotional support in the midst of her own labors.

Author's Note

The identities of the people written about in this book have been carefully disguised in accordance with professional standards of confidentiality and in keeping with their rights to privileged communication with the author.

Introduction

When a social worker's client who is receiving help for a marital problem or a guidance counselor's student who is having behavior or academic problems begins to talk about his or her religious feelings, beliefs, or attitudes, it is easy to regard the introduction of this material as a digression (or resistance). If the client or student's religion is familiar and of interest, the professional may readily be drawn into a discussion, argument, or even a friendly agreement about the religious topic the client has introduced. The professional nature of the work can well be derailed, or at least delayed. Perhaps the counselor or social worker, recognizing the danger ahead, changes the topic or even says that he or she does not discuss religion or politics. The work may go on without any realization of the loss of potentially important—and professionally relevant—thoughts, attitudes, and feelings. Thinking that such material is a direct expression of spiritual values, or that this is an alternative way to bring about desirable change, the professional may take up the ideas or feelings the student or client offers without realizing that this material expresses complex and often conflicting motives.

But if a student or client's religious views are professionally relevant, how can this be dealt with? Don't you risk intruding into a highly personal area? Is not the school or agency (particularly if state or federally funded) at risk for accusations of violation of church-and-state separation? These are serious questions which this book will try to answer in detail. Briefly however, consider the following situation:

Mrs. A is depressed and is seeing a social worker. Quickly enough the social worker recognizes that the depression is a symptom of Mrs. A's anger at her husband who is domineering, unresponsive to her needs for emotional support, and unhelpful in raising their children. Efforts to bring this anger to the client's awareness are opposed until finally the client "explains" that anger is not acceptable. Jesus says to turn the other cheek and Paul declares that wives must submit to their husbands. If the social worker argues with Mrs. A, the client again has the experience of being dominated and not being listened to sensitively. If this obstacle is not dealt with out of respect for the client's religion (which is considered "off limits"), Mrs. A's depression is likely to persist. What to do?

Without allowing oneself to be drawn into an argument over the validity of these convictions as a way to construct a marriage, the client can be invited to elaborate on her beliefs about marriage. This can then lead to Mrs. A describing her parents' marriage and her mother's relationship with her father. If this opens up the kind of useful therapeutic material needed to free up Mrs. A, then the salience of this single tenet about wives and marriage, selected out of a very diverse and complex mosaic of ideas, may recede and counseling can proceed. But perhaps this procedure does not help. There are options, such as investigating in a collaborative way with Mrs. A where these statements appear in the Bible and in what context, or what are alternative meanings and translations. How to do this will be dealt with in chapters 5 and 6.

Let us look at another situation:

The parents of a high school student contact a guidance counselor because James' schoolwork has been steadily declining. Suspecting drug or alcohol abuse, the counselor secures teacher reports on the student's classroom deportment but these do not show the changes consistent with alcohol or drug abuse. In conference with the parents, another strong concern emerges when the parents express their perplexity and distress over their son's recent involvement in a small religious group, which they call a cult, now active in the school. In essence they are saying, "My son has been stolen by trolls." This group is affiliated with a local church recently established by a dynamic minister who had broken away from a large church in town that was part of a mainline denomination. If the guidance counselor fears to comment because of school board policy prohibiting school officials from involvement in religious activities, James' schoolwork will likely continue to decline. Sympathizing with the parents' distress and perhaps even suggesting ways to intervene to pull their son away from this "cult," and offering to find additional tutoring for James is unlikely to do more than intensify the stress between James and his parents. What to do? Before sketching an answer, let us consider religion in the United States.

In most countries, even where religion is not regulated by the government, there is one, or perhaps two dominant religions. The other religions are typically much smaller in membership. In contrast, most parts of the United States offer Americans a "smorgasbord" of religions, divided by ethnic origins, doctrinal differences, emotional expressiveness, and a host of other factors. Individual spirituality, more or less unconnected with a specific denomination, church, or sect is another dimension that characterizes religious experiences in the United States. Nevertheless when people say that they are Catholic, Baptist, Lutheran, Episcopalian, or Jewish, others who are not intimately knowledgeable about that denomination may assume that they understand what that means. Nothing could be a more misleading assumption! I deliberately mentioned five denominations for this illustration that are particularly diverse, but to greater or lesser degrees diversity is characteristic of all denominations.

What are the implications of such diversity? Firstly it means that people have a great deal more choice and *making* such a choice is likely to enhance commitment. Thus Americans are more likely to attend church, to have a higher degree of interest in religion, and are more likely to express a belief in a Supreme Being or God than is true of many countries (particularly in Western Europe).[1] Moreover, churchgoers include both younger and older people and sex distributions are likely to be more even. Religion in the United States engages more than the elderly women usually thought of as primary churchgoers.[2] Involvement in religious activities through church activities, church-based political action, informal study groups, seminary study, and entry into the ministry are all much more common in the United States. Thus religion is an important activity and people influence the form, structure, and expression of religious activities.

One example of this involvement is the Roman Catholic practice of offering wine during the Eucharist to all in the congregation who wish to participate during the Mass. The Vatican had attempted to stop this practice, assuming that an improper commotion would occur. It took some serious discussion before the Vatican realized that the commotion that would be common in an Italian church would not occur in an American church where people would line up quietly. Another example of the level of lay involvement with their church is seen in the Catholic Church again. There is a shortage of priests in many parts of the world and a decline in religious vocations (i.e., nuns and monks). However this is much less true in the United States than in Western Europe.

To the extent that religions involve the whole person they are congruent with important personality and cognitive functions. Thus, religious choice expresses significant aspects of both the person's current personality organization and formative developmental experiences in his or her life. And because there is so much diversity, even staying with the religion of one's family is a choice for many people. When the person who keeps the family's religion does not experience any choice, that person's autonomy may be seriously limited. However, there are communities (e.g., Amish) where the child-rearing is such that autonomy may not be an issue. Hence behavior must also be refracted through the norms of the family, religion, and community.

To return to the problem of James and his parents, it is first important to note that the term *cult* is frequently applied to a religious group we disapprove of. This is not an accurate usage and we will give better ones in chapter 1. The counselor may begin by asking about the family, James' role and place among his siblings, and the family's religious attitude and orientation. What might emerge is that James is the oldest of four children in a thoroughly secular family with high standards and expectations for all their children. One possible understanding is that James is attempting to define his own identity and to "get his parents off his back" by taking a very different stance. Another is that James feels poorly connected to his parents except through what he accomplishes. The dynamic minister in the breakaway church has become a warm and accepting father who cares about James' thoughts and feelings (his soul) rather than his exterior accomplishments. Either of these understandings points to useful and appropriate topics to explore with the family that will be consistent with the needs of both the student and his family. These understandings neither refuse to explore the parents' religious views nor support the parents in a way that will impair a resolution of their problem and concerns.

In essence this book sees religion as very important

in the lives of many people, expressing complex and often competing motives, wishes, and interests both within people and between people and their family and social environment. When religious themes arise in the course of professional work, one may understand these themes in several ways. I hear these themes as people expressing important aspects of their past or present experiences, but in a religious idiom. The person is telling me useful things about his or her world, but not in plain English. To translate what the client or student is saying into plainer English is one goal of this book. A second goal is to give the counselor alternative ways to understand and respond to the client's concerns in a helpful manner. A third goal is to challenge counselors to reflect on what religion means personally so as to try to avoid professional activities that come more from one's private needs than those of the client. Finally I want to provide information about many of the significant religious denominations and movements found in this country, including cults. In addition, this book also tackles a number of religious concepts and terms which are relevant to the work of professionals.

Some cautionary notes about reading this book are in order here. When I discuss clergy in general (minister, priest, rabbi, imam) I will typically use clergy, minister, and sometimes pastor. Where a specific denomination is being considered, the standard label will be used. Religion deeply touches many people in a most personal way, both positively and negatively. My approach is a special kind of objectivity. Sometimes objective means to have no feelings or values. This is often impossible and it is frequently deceptive to try to pretend to this state. Rather, my position is objective in the sense of fostering self-awareness of competing tugs exerted by various aspects of the topic, and also in attempting to inquire into the multiple meanings that are possible in any complex system of thought and feeling. Readers who incline toward a religious orientation may find this a cold position, but I am trying to model what I find professionally useful. Non-religious readers may wonder why I am more positive about religion than they believe is realistic. To both I say that the best test of this approach is to study and test it out. Belief is not necessary in order to try it.

1

The Helping Professions and Religion

Ministry, Counseling, and Psychotherapy

A marital couple I had seen on and off for a period of time returned for further counseling. In the interim, the wife had consulted a Catholic priest in her area who had a good reputation for work with married couples. Some of his counseling was reportedly at odds with my work with the couple and it would have been easy to feel resentment over his "interference." It would have been a mistake to allow the wife's report to set up a competition between the priest and myself and thus interfere with the counseling work we were doing. The counseling function of the priest is ancient and is described in the Bible,[1] while advice giving appears in the Wisdom literature (Proverbs, Ecclesiastes, Ecclesiasticus or Ben Sira), as do seers and witches. It is easy to "put down" such ancient counseling as nonscientific, or to see only the similarities, concluding that the Bible "has it all" and that this or other ancient traditions[2] make modern methods superfluous.

Neither approach does justice to both the similarities and the differences between past and present. The Wisdom[3] literature, with its accumulated sayings, summarizes different writers' perception of human motivation, society, and advice for living a good life. Their recommendations on relations with others may offer acute advice or destructive interventions. Twentieth century scientific prescriptions from John B. Watson to Dr. Spock span a similar range. The ancient writings differ from modern ones in how they are understood. Ancient writings are seen as divinely inspired while modern writings are open to revision based on experience or research. A second difference is based on the understanding of intervention. Ancient writings tended to be descriptive as in:

> "Careless work makes a man poor,
> Whereas diligent effort brings wealth."[4]

or prescriptive as in:

> "He who will not punish his son shows no love
> for him,
> For if he love him he should be concerned to
> discipline him."[5]

Modern approaches to emotional and behavioral problems deal with abstractions (theories) while Scripture is concrete in language and imagery. Abstractions are dealt with in the Hebrew text,[6] but through the use of concrete images. Modern methods usually deal with the *process* of intervention which is absent from the Bible. Modern approaches make the therapeutic relationship explicit; the person's development of an internally directed position is a highly valued goal in the modern world. In the biblical world the concept of a single, self-directing, self-aware individual was nearly inconceivable.[7] The emphasis was on the community, which was the primary unit that was either favored or punished by God. Another crucial difference between modern and biblical approaches is the much more open-ended nature of psychological theorizing, which is subject to modification through empirical research and theory development.

In the earlier part of this century the counseling function of the clergy was downplayed in many seminary programs, which instead focused on technical preparation in Scripture, theology, apologetics and homiletics. Ministers in congregations who were called on to counsel were performing ancient functions for which they were no longer trained and which most knew were provided by secular professionals. There was often considerable interprofessional rivalry that still has not completely abated. The omission of counseling training has been largely reversed and many clergy now receive much more substantial training in counseling and psychotherapy,[8] including applied experiences in prisons, hospitals, and other relevant settings. Some clergy practice psychoanalysis, psychotherapy, social work, or counseling in a variety of settings.[9] While rivalry still remains, some basis for cooperative endeavors exists, as both ministerial and secular counselors serve at least partly reciprocal functions.

The situation is perhaps somewhat less rosy in graduate training programs, as an increasing number of overtly religious candidates are in training for social work, counseling and clinical psychology. Faculty on student admissions committees typically were trained when there was more antagonism between psychology and religion. They are more likely to view such students with doubt and may be wary of candidates whose minds they suspect of being closed and biased. Further, the training of older faculty was often deficient in the objective study of religion.[10]

Some Problems Posed by Religious Themes in Counseling

There are a variety of difficulties posed when a counselee raises a theme with religious content or connotations. Although these have been discussed elsewhere,[11] a number of these will be discussed in this book.

The Counselor's Personal Contribution

The common avoidance of religious or political conversations is rooted in the recognition that these topics generate strong, even intense reactions. It is nearly impossible to grow up in this society without exposure to religion and without some feelings about it. When we are taught about religion as children, it is presented in a concrete manner, suitable to the understanding of the child. Sometimes the punitive aspects are prominent. Religion is often sanitized so as not to generate embarrassing questions. Abstract thinking flowers in adolescence, at about the time that most people discontinue religious instruction so they are often left with the feeling that religion is childish and punitive.

As one pastoral therapist put it "No one who had a childhood has a liberal theology."[12] A graduate student of mine who had grown up as a Catholic but who no longer attended church or felt affiliated with her Catholic upbringing told me, with some amusement, of her horrified reaction to seeing a news story on a tasteless (if not vulgar) movie about Mary. She ruefully commented that "you can take the girl out of the Catholic, but you can't take the Catholic out of the girl."

Those raised in a household with values and attitudes antagonistic to religion are no more neutral. Even the professional raised in a home where the parents were relatively indifferent to religion was first a child who in all likelihood had to face other children who posed questions about religious affiliation. When other children ask what church or synagogue you go to, saying you are not "something" when other children *are* "something" is uncomfortable.

How does this complex history, which differs from one person to another, affect the professional counselor, teacher, or social worker? Basically, the effect is to set up conditions that frequently influence the person's attitudes, feelings and behaviors. For example:

A social worker I supervised while she was studying for an advanced degree worked with a woman raised in a Christian Science home by a domineering but distant mother. The client, an isolated and frustrated woman, had few relationships and little satisfaction from them. Over time, the client was able to improve the quality of her relationships through treatment. After a summer vacation, the social worker returned to receive the client's disconcerting announcement that she was born again, having received Christ as her savior. The social worker's reactions were clearly negative even after I pointed out that the client now had a relation with *someone* (i.e., Jesus). Exploration with another supervisor revealed that the social worker grew up in a Jewish home with one older brother whom the parents favored, and called "the Messiah." (*Mashiach* in Hebrew is translated in Greek as *Christos*.) Once she was able to see how her secondary position in her own family and the particular way in which the brother was characterized by her parents impacted upon her attitudes, she was able to reassume a professional attitude and accept the client's relationship to Jesus.[13]

Other common ways to avoid the feelings aroused by the appearance of religious themes in counseling include indicating that this is not within the range of acceptable topics; it is personal, like politics. Counseling deals with personal matters and the counselor cannot know if the material is relevant without exploring it. Thus negative reactions, such as that given in the example above, or ignoring religious themes, or indicating they are off limits, will all interfere with the exploration and resolution that counseling makes possible. There is another, more subtle way the counselor can act that clouds the counseling process. This is to become enthusiastically interested in, and supportive of, the client's religious expression, thus missing the underlying meanings which may be quite different from the surface ones.

Cult, Sect and Church

"Cult" is usually a disparaging term applied to a religious group that is: "(1) unconventional and esoteric; (2) controversial and the target of allegations of harmful acts; (3) authoritarian; (4) close-knit and communal; (5) aggressively proselytizing; (6) intense and emotional in its indoctrination practices or group ritual; and (7) charismatic in its leadership."[14] Some writers distinguish between cults and destructive cults. Hare Krishna, The Way, The Unification Church, Church of Scientology, and the Children of God are groups often consigned to the category of "destructive cults." This will be clarified in chapter 4.

There are other meanings to the term cult. In official Roman Catholic practice it does not have negative connotations but refers to a special interest among some Church members. Thus the "Cult of Mary" signifies a special way of honoring Mary, the mother of Jesus.

Labels that stigmatize what we dislike or fear relieve us of the burden of thinking seriously about a problem. The terminology used here comes from sociological literature and does not stigmatize. *Cult* refers to a religious group that arises more or less spontaneously, that is, not directly from a church. Christian Science and The Church of Jesus Christ of Latter-Day Saints are two examples of churches that began as cults. A *sect* begins as a group within an ongoing church, such as the Methodists, who began within the Church of England before they separated out. Christianity began as a Jewish sect. Sects tend to withdraw from the surrounding social environment, while churches accept their social environment. When a sect opens to the world it becomes a church.

The Secular Origins of Counseling and Psychotherapy

Counseling and psychotherapy had quite different origins, although many people confuse the two disciplines. Modern secular counseling probably originated in 1898 with the work of Jesse Davis with Detroit high school students with educational and vocational problems. Some ten years later Frank Parsons founded a vocational bureau in Boston. The following year this bureau began work in the Boston schools. Soon other cities developed similar systems. The development of standardized ability tests, arising from the study of individual differences, was a very important contributor to the development of counseling, which initially focused on educational decisions.

Psychotherapy began with the work of Sigmund Freud and, at one time, psychoanalysis was the only form of psychotherapy. Many knowledgeable people know that Freud was anti-religious. Some see him as nearly satanic.[15] Because of the equation that many make between psychoanalysis, psychotherapy and counseling, many clients and not a few counselors or social workers who are personally religious may hold antagonistic attitudes toward counseling, psychotherapy, or more specifically to Freud's ideas.

The reality of Freud's views is both more interesting and more complex. Freud was very good friends with Oskar Pfister, a well-known Swiss clergyman who, after Freud wrote *The Future of an Illusion*, wrote a critique in *The Illusion of a Future* at Freud's request. In several of his papers and books Freud noted parallels between various patterns of emotional disturbance and similar distortions of religious thought and feelings. Obsessive doubting or scrupulosity (which afflicted Martin Luther among others) is only one such parallel. It was Pfister who declared "Tell me what you find in the Bible, and I will tell you what you are."[16] In *The Future of an Illusion* Freud did not hold that religion was false, but that it contained significant wishes. A careful reading of his writings shows that although he was not religious he respected "the mighty personality of religious doctrines,"[17] but had little regard for intellectual games masquerading as theology.

Actually Freud's views on religion are irrelevant to his ideas about the nature of human development, about the multifaceted ways in which the person's growth can be distorted, stunted, channeled and enhanced, and filled with conflicting fears, ambitions, meanings, and motives. For religious clients, faced with the frightening challenge of counseling, burdened with warnings about the danger to their salvation that counseling poses, and guilty that their commitment to their faith did not protect them from emotional problems,[18] a fuller understanding of Freud and religion is irrelevant. If clients can express their fears, or if the counselor can guess at them accurately, then it is possible to start to deal with these anxieties. We will come back to this more fully later, but in brief, I find that a neutral but interested stance serves me best. If I am asked directly about my religious orientation (Am I saved? Am I a Christian? Will counseling tear me [the client] away from my faith? and so on), I try to answer honestly. If I sense that the client can tolerate being put off temporarily I will say something like, "Before I answer your question, could we explore what this means to you?"

Most clients who have screwed up their courage to confront a stranger on so sensitive a topic will not be able to hear such a question as an ordinary probe in counseling and will be better served by an answer such as, "I want to answer your question, but then I would like to hear how you feel about what I have to say." I then say that I am Jewish and I do not think that my purpose is to change their faith, but only to help them with the difficulties in life that have brought them here. They are frequently relieved to hear that the counselor can speak simply and directly and may spontaneously declare their fears. If needed, the counselor may also point out that many of the people clients work with are not of their persuasion, or that their physician may not be saved and yet can render valuable assistance. One may present counseling in that light.

But perhaps the therapist *is* a Christian (in the sense of having been saved, or accepted Jesus as a personal savior). The client may express relief, and the counselor is tempted to take the acceptance offered as a gift. But here too, the failure to be clear and open at the outset about the need to explore various issues may well lead to eventual dissatisfaction when the counselor falls short in some way, or has to inquire into the client's particular meanings. Without being intimidating, the counselor will usually be in a clearer position if he or she indicates that because they share a similar faith position, this does not mean that certain areas will never be discussed.

Overlaps and Contrasts Between Counseling, Psychotherapy, and Ministry

Both counseling and psychotherapy are extremely diverse within each field. Surveying several books on counseling theories and methods, one finds they range from psychoanalytic, client-centered, and behavioral theories and techniques to extensive discussions of career counseling, theories of vocational choice and educational, vocational, and interest tests. Psychotherapy texts also cover a spectrum, so one may ask what is meant here by psychotherapy and by counseling: how are they similar and how are they different?

There are perhaps three main trends in counseling. The first is counseling to assist a person with an educational, vocational or personal problem by assembling relevant information, resources, and specialized advice or data. The second is counseling as a personal interaction between the parties to aid the counselee to resolve a problem or meet needs. Many counselors tend to assume that their clients are not mentally disturbed and the counselor's task is to aid the client to choose or revise goals, plan for the present or future, develop or enhance skills, or alter behavior.[19] A third trend sees counseling as not so distinct from psychotherapy, except by the degree to which deep personal change is a main goal.

Psychotherapy may well be defined in a way similar to the second or third of these definitions, which emphasize the professional use of the relationship to help reach the client's personal goal; but in psychotherapy the client (or patient) is seen as having more serious difficulties. More attention may be paid to the expression of intense emotion, the details of the person's thoughts about the world or the self, recovery of memory and feelings about past experiences, and examining the nature and meaning of the interaction between client and therapist, or between the client and important persons in the client's environment. Many counselors would not see much difference between counseling and psychotherapy, so the similarities and differences depend on the personal view of the counselor or psychotherapist. Even if the work is similar, counseling is a much less intimidating term than psychotherapy and definitions seem much a matter of individual preference.

Definitions of ministry are equally complex, but a traditional view, consistent with American usage, sees ministry as encompassing the ritual or liturgical activities of the priest, minister, or rabbi. The minister meets the spiritual needs of the congregants through a variety of specific activities, including study, preaching (teaching), advising (counseling), spiritual direction (therapy), and comforting (support), with a ritual practice consistent with the custom of the denomination. A key concept here is *spiritual.* The parenthetic comments just above parallel secular counseling with ministry in the emotional life of the person, plus a felt connection between the person and something transcendent (God, Spirit, the Divine, the Presence, and so on).

Recent developments in many churches (particularly the more sacramental denominations) point toward an expanding involvement of parishioners (laity) in a variety of liturgical and administrative functions, and an increasingly prominent view of ministry as much more than just liturgical. Ministry is also being defined in an action sense, aimed toward social justice, freeing people in both material and emotional ways. Of course there are other churches that have had this emphasis for a long time, such as the Methodists, Seventh-Day Adventists, and Society of Friends (Quakers).

One apparent distinction between ministry and counseling or psychotherapy is the clear presence of an articulated and elaborated moral code. Many professional and nonprofessional persons would subscribe to the concept that counseling or psychotherapy is relatively or completely value-free, while ministry emphasizes a moral code. In terms of professional functioning, all three domains have clear-cut ethical codes. Counselors and psychotherapists usually appear nonjudgmental to the client to enable the client to disclose those experiences, feelings, wishes, and actions that must be divulged to permit their work to go forward. Values are nevertheless implicit in this work since the goal is to enable the client to be honest with himself or herself.[20] That which can not be faced can not be changed.

In ministerial counseling, invoking moral imperatives, perhaps when the minister is deeply offended by a person's behavior. or is puzzled as to what else to do, may be initially attractive. If this works successfully, the minister may not discover that the parishioner has come for punishment, which suppresses the problem but may not allow the energies involved in the problem area to be released for more creative uses. When people who consult a minister find that they will be accepted and heard nonjudgmentally, this can be immensely freeing and healing. Some minister-counselors adhere strictly to counseling neutrality in the customary sense.

The Development of Religions in America

When I was in grade school in New York City, we had regular assemblies where a teacher would read some selection from the Bible. I had no understanding of what was being read, so I ignored it as, I suspect, did most of my classmates. Yet in retrospect such readings reflected how substantially religion was woven into American civic life. Today many people believe that religion has been extracted from public life and feel that this is a bad (or good) thing. The notion that religion is now excluded from American life is incorrect since the United States remains a society in which religion is powerfully important, particularly compared to the rest of the Western world. G. K. Chesterton's remark that the United States is a "nation with the soul of a church" is worth repeating here.[21] In many Western countries, a particular denomination is either the established religion, which gives it certain political advantages at the price of substantial disinterest among the populace, or the country has disestablished its church and maintains a hostile attitude toward religion.

Since the United States was founded it has not had an established church, yet paradoxically there has been a powerful, continuing flowering of religious interest, movements, and sects. Some of these movements and sects have grown into churches, although others have withered. To the casual observer, it is hard to detect much order in this chaos. What follows is a very condensed sketch of how the major church groups arose and where they stand in relation to each other in American life today.

A Brief Historical Survey

While there are other powerful and significant religions in the world, this discussion will focus primarily on Judaism and Christianity, with some attention to Islam.[22] This choice is dictated by the North American locus of this book and the likelihood that a counselor will see someone with a background in one of these three main religions.

There are many definitions of religion, several of which will be offered here. A simple one holds religion to be "a system of beliefs in a divine or superhuman power, and practices of worship or other rituals directed towards such a power."[23] Another, related view is that:

1. Religion is a structured pattern of relations (beliefs and rituals) to some divine (superhuman, other-worldly) power(s),
2. Religion is centrally concerned with ethical relations among individuals and groups in society.[24]

Another way to state this is in terms of the relationship one has with the meanings of one's life,[25] which takes this out of a formal religious setting. Sometimes other activities, including political allegiances or philosophical systems are defined as religions. To regard these as religions does violence to the term, but to apply the term religion expresses that other human activities use human processes similar to those of religion. Sociologically, religion is often characterized as "a stable cluster of values, norms, statuses, roles, and groups developed around a basic social need. . .[with] particular attention to how patterns of religious belief and practice vary and under what social structural conditions these variations occur."[26]

All these definitions include *belief* as a component of religion. In this sense, Judaism differs partly from Islam and quite substantially from Christianity. Judaism is the culture of a people founded on God's promise of a land (Canaan) to live in, contingent upon their fulfillment of the contractual (covenantal) relationship between the Israelites and God. In this covenant the children of Israel (Jacob) agree to live their lives in accord with a moral/ritual code. What they will receive, and the penalties for breaking the agreement are also set forth. While there are beliefs in Judaism, there is no agreed-upon creed or confession of faith. Even the thirteen principles of belief put forth by Maimonides,[27] while given great respect, were not universally accepted as articles of faith. Thus Jewish life is based on a community organized around a detailed and complex pattern of ritual and ethical behaviors that permeates the lives of those who live Judaism fully. Nevertheless, belief and hope exist and serve as a glue to bind scattered communities in a shared promise of a positive future.

It was a well-developed culture some thousand or more years old that Jesus was born into, for the first followers of Jesus were all Jews and many were associated with, or attracted to the teachings and practices of the Pharisees.[28] Two branches of Jesus' teachings grew up after his death. The one that continued within Judaism likely perished in the general disaster of the first Jewish rebellion ending with the fall of Jerusalem in 70 C.E.[29] The other branch, which St. Paul allied himself with, formed the early Christian Church. Our knowledge of these formative years is incomplete, but we know that there were diverse, strongly competing beliefs and the Church that eventually emerged when Christianity became the official religion of the Roman Empire was not the only possible path. Nor was the Church's development finished.

Central to Christian thought are three concepts: Creation, Redemption, and Resurrection.[30] While this is not the only way to construe or organize these concepts, Creation refers to the idea that the world and humanity are God's doing and without that foundational act, nothing would follow. Further, the world is good[31] even if people were not able to maintain that quality of goodness within themselves. They needed Redemption through God's presence in the world in the person of Jesus, whose death was an atoning act to provide a path for reconciliation with God. God is present to human beings through multiple facets (the Trinity). The Resurrection's central theme is not that Jesus was brought back to life but that God is faithful to humanity, even in death. Thus Christianity in its many forms is fully a religion since it is a systematized pattern of beliefs and faith, fortified by ritual, behavioral, and ethical practices.

Islam comes from a word meaning peace (*salaam*) but secondarily surrender or submission (to God's will). It contains both clearly stated beliefs, organized and systematically set forth in the *Qur'an*[32] as dictated by Muhammad, and practices set within a community and organized within a code called the *Shari'a*. There are six central beliefs:

1. one God,
2. angels who act as God's agents,
3. books, including Jewish and Christian Scripture which are now regarded as no longer present in the original, having been corrupted by Jews and Christians,
4. prophets or messengers, most of whom are described in the Bible, and Jesus as one of the most important,
5. a Day of Judgment, and
6. predestination; all that occurs is God's will.[33]

Further, while not on a level of full equality with Muslims, Jews and Christians are protected (*dhimmi*) within Islam as peoples who worship one God, believe in a messenger and a book. Islam has been largely invisible in this country and is generally regarded negatively because of its association with Iran and terrorism. Paradoxically, compared with Judaism and Christianity, Islam takes the strongest position on charitable responsibility for those who are in need, and on equality between men and women, mandating modest dress for *both* sexes for example. It is currently undergoing rapid growth in the United States, with about four and one-half million adherents, offering a pious, austere but satisfying life. The group once known as the Black Muslims was considered deviant from normative Islam but has now come into the mainstream and forms an important segment of the Islamic community in the United States.[34]

The separation of the one community into the modern Jewish and Christian divisions was a protracted process. Some of the polemics against Jews by early Christian writers were perhaps in part to protect a smaller, more fragile community from reabsorption. Even later the tendency of some Christians to "fraternize" aroused recurrent anxiety. A drift from Jewish to Christian affiliation also occurred, kindling similar concerns. The early Christian Church split into two main divisions in 1054 C.E., nominally over a difference in their view of the Trinity that is today so esoteric that hardly any parishioners in either tradition could define it. The Eastern Orthodox church tended toward a mystical, emotional quality in its religious thought and observances, while the Roman Catholic church inclined toward a more cognitive, rational character.[35] Other differences also exist, including the structure of the sacrament of reconciliation (penance), marriage for priests, anointing the sick and the role of the Patriarch vs. that of the Pope. The Roman Catholic church has increased in both numbers and proportion of the world's population while the Eastern Orthodox church has hardly grown in numbers in this century, thus declining in proportion to the world's population.[36]

The Roman Catholic church came to dominate Western Europe until the fractures that developed around the time of the Reformation. While he was not the first to raise serious questions, when Luther nailed his theses to the door of the church of the Wittenberg Castle he had not intended to break with Rome, but to debate and reform some dubious church practices (many of which were later altered in the Counter-Reformation). Shortly after Luther's act, theological and political forces already simmering below the surface exploded into open revolt. This was followed by the Presbyterian movement in Switzerland, led by Zwingli and Calvin, which diverged somewhat further from Roman Catholicism and was closer to the Radical Reformation. The latter included such groups as the Amish, Mennonite, and Baptist. These churches tended to turn away from the wider world and avoided contact with rulers (the government) and government activities, such as military service.

The break between Rome and England came later, stimulated by Henry VIII's driving need for an annulment in order to remarry to produce a male heir. He had a strong interest in theological matters and was given the title "Defender of the Faith" for opposing Protestantism. Thus the Anglican church was closer to the Roman Catholic church in many matters, although priests were allowed to marry. In this country, the Church of England is the Episcopal church and is regarded as Protestant.

The evolution of the various Christian churches may be easier to see in Figure 1 which traces the main lines of development of the Christian churches, both in Europe and this country. As may be seen, many of the churches in the United States, from the Amish to the Society of Friends (Quakers), had their beginnings in Europe. This diagram, while not complete, includes most of the major denominations. The internal diversity of many denominations is also not represented. For example, Baptist, Lutheran, and Episcopal are three highly diverse churches under their denominational umbrellas, while Holiness and Pentecostal churches are often individualistic and loosely affiliated.

Thus many of the major denominations arose from the Roman Catholic church, often reflecting a specific facet of the Church. For example the Amish and Mennonite churches tend to be closed groups, emphasizing work, community and an enthusiastic spirituality, similar to that of monastic communities. The Lutheran church sees salvation as completely dependent on faith and on God's grace, but good deeds are desirable indicators of such grace.

FIGURE 1
Developmental Lines of the Main American Christian Denominations

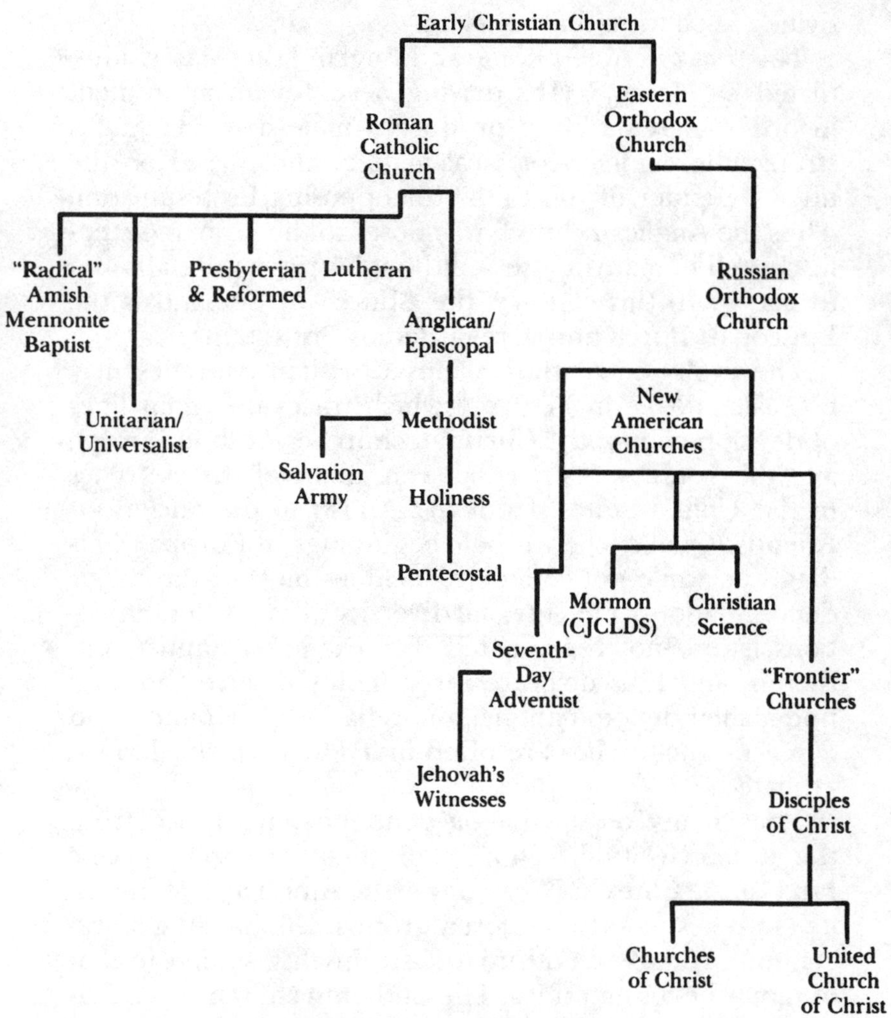

A good deal of Catholic ritual and sacrament is retained, as is a parochial school system and emphasis on social services.

American Black Churches

Christianity had a slow start among black slaves brought to the Colonies in the first 120 years, partly due to opposition by owners who felt it made the slaves troublesome and inclined to think better of themselves. With the general religious revivalism that spread through the colonies in the 1740s, more slaves were converted to Christianity, once the Anglican emphasis on study and reading was superseded by the Presbyterian, Methodist, and Baptist emphasis on direct conversion experiences. After a time, Methodist and Baptist clergymen began to license black men to preach and these preachers converted and ministered directly to black people without white intervention. Even though increasing numbers of slaves were introduced to Christianity, many blacks were not church-affiliated by the time of the emancipation in 1863. Most blacks attended church with whites before the Civil War, although some black churches date to before the Revolution. Many whites, both in the North and South, were not pleased by the presence of black churches, which were the only institutions over which blacks exercised control. These churches were the seedbeds of black leadership during and after slavery.

Efforts by whites to secure control over black churches and their property led to court battles in which blacks successfully beat off these attempts. These white efforts mobilized blacks, and in 1816 the African Methodist Episcopal Church was organized. Shortly thereafter two other denominations were established.

> As centers of social, economic, educational, and political life, these churches formed the institutional core

> for the development of free black communities in the North. They also formed a platform from which black leaders, frequently the ministers themselves, addressed the issues confronting their people.[37]

Between the Civil War and World War I, conditions deteriorated for blacks in many ways, but the black churches throughout the country served as focal points for leadership and ameliorative activities. The founding of black educational institutes (e.g., Tuskegee Institute) and black self-help agencies (e.g., NAACP) broadened the leadership base for social, educational, economic, and political improvement. Although black Protestant churches were increasingly criticized for their withdrawal from black political problems in the mid-twentieth century, the support of black pastors was often crucial to the organizing efforts of the NAACP and similar organizations. Nevertheless, when the Montgomery bus boycott was organized, Baptist minister Martin Luther King, Jr. was asked to be spokesman. His practical and philosophical positions were not fully accepted within the black community and the slow pace of black gains gave Malcolm X's criticisms increasing point. The alternative presented by the American Moslem Mission (Black Muslims) was also attractive even though the majority of black Americans with a church affiliation were connected with black Protestant churches. Recently black churches have been again actively addressing the needs of the community through programs (such as Project SPIRIT) aimed at improving the preparation of black children in school, reducing the damage caused by early pregnancies and young, single-parent families, and enhancing parent effectiveness.[38]

While there were black Catholics before the Revolution, Catholicism had a slower start among blacks than did Protestantism. The first black priest was not ordained in the United States until 1891. In spite of this, the Catholic Church has been increasing its black membership and its emphasis on universalism is attractive to some blacks.

American Indigenous Churches

It is not possible to survey all the churches the United States has given rise to here, but several of the most important should be noted. The Mormons (derisively named after one of their important Scriptural additions), or The Church of Jesus Christ of Latter-Day Saints, as they are properly known, developed in the 1820s. This was primarily the work of Joseph Smith, who founded it on a new scriptural revelation (*The Book of Mormon*) given to him by the angel Moroni. The little group that formed around Joseph Smith as a prophet in upper New York State went "public" in 1830 with six elders and about fifty members. His claim to prophecy may have been less important initially than his assertion to be the only true Christian church.[39] The group grew and moved several times, until much turmoil led to the murder of Joseph Smith in 1844, followed by a major exodus to Utah under the leadership of Brigham Young in 1847. After a long period of isolated development, intense political pressure led to abandoning theocratic practices offensive to the majority of non-Mormons, and relinquishing polygamy. The Church of Jesus Christ of Latter-Day Saints began to enter the mainstream of American church life. The history of the Latter-Day Saints shows the progressive changes from cult to church.

The next major church to develop in the first half of the nineteenth century was the Seventh-Day Adventists. Rooted in apocalyptic Scripture (Daniel, Revelation), with intense hopes for the return of Christ, people were stimulated by the prediction by William Miller that Christ's return would happen in March of 1843. When this did not happen, Miller's figures were recalculated to March,

1844 and then to October, 1844. The repetitive failures should have led to the complete dispersal of the group, but instead Miller and a faithful remnant reorganized and formed an ongoing, congregational structure. Eventually they deduced that Miller's predictions had indeed begun, but in Heaven. Ellen White and her husband James rose to positions of leadership. Mrs. White and Mary Baker Eddy are two of the very few women to have founded a major denomination in this country. She issued a considerable body of secondary literature that formed an additional Scriptural canon. The Adventists developed divergent practices that did not arouse nearly the same ire the Latter-Day Saints faced. The Sabbath was observed on Saturday instead of Sunday, and dietary practices resembled those described in the Old Testament, at least as it pertained to butchering animals (kosher meat is used if available). Modern American concerns about diet have their roots in the welter of movements that arose at that time. Evangelist Sylvester Graham (now remembered for his crackers) and Dr. John Kellogg (who invented corn flakes) were connected with these trends and interests.[40]

If the Seventh-Day Adventists were co-founded by a husband-and-wife team, Christian Science was the work of one woman, Mary Baker Eddy. Utilizing an idea she acquired from Phineas Quimby in 1862—that illness arises from incorrect thinking—Eddy developed an elaborate system of theology and healing which she presented in 1875 when she published *Science and Health with Key to the Scriptures*. By the end of that decade she established the Church of Christ, Scientist in Boston. This church still controls the activities of the denomination in considerable detail. To outsiders, medical treatment only through prayer (except for setting broken bones) is the most striking feature of Christian Science. When one considers the perilous nature of medical treatment until well into the twentieth century, Eddy's approach had something to recommend it. At the least it accords with the medical maxim: First, do no harm. In her concern for health, Mary Baker Eddy was well within the general spirit of her time and all three of the denominations that we have just considered (Mormons, Adventists, Christian Scientists) emphasized, in differing ways, the value of naturalistic or spiritual approaches to healing and health.

At about the same time as Mary Baker Eddy founded Christian Science, Charles Russell felt distressed over his religious doubts about the Bible but found that Adventist beliefs were of help. He began to issue a series of writings, to aid in the study of the Bible, which proposed a radical view of standard Christian doctrines, including a rejection of the Trinity, and a complex series of apocalyptic visions dating cataclysmic future events. His successor Joseph Rutherford effectively developed an organization to promote Russell's views. The Jehovah's Witnesses (Watchtower Society) were organized into groups called Kingdom Halls, since churches were rejected as satanic devices. This, plus their rejection of military service, intense anti-Catholicism, refusal to allow their children to recite the Pledge of Allegiance, the prohibition of blood transfusions promulgated in 1945 (as eating blood, which is prohibited in the Old Testament), and aggressive proselytizing made the Witnesses the object of considerable discrimination and persecution.

The last set of churches to be considered here are the "frontier" churches: a group of mainstream, moderately conservative churches that arose out of an effort to reunify Protestant denominations. These churches, including the Churches of Christ, Disciples of Christ (or Christian Church), and the United Church of Christ, arose mainly at the frontier and did not develop creedal or hierarchical structures that would foster division or schism. Even so, the Churches of Christ separated from the Disciples of Christ at the start of this century.[41] Although homegrown, these churches are rooted in mainline Protestant thought and are moderately diverse in theological and political terms.

The story of religious developments in the United States is far from finished. Any account of the recent developments and controversies over new cults, sects, and churches would be soon outdated, as would a study of the struggles and disputes over teaching Creationism, access to abortion, clergy running for high public office, and prayer in the public schools. The purpose here is to sketch the bare historical developments, leaving the theological underpinnings aside until the next chapter, where their implications for the counseling process will be discussed.

2

American Religions and Their Implications for Counseling

The Structure of Counseling

Some parallels between counseling, psychotherapy, and ministry were suggested in the previous chapter, but I am not asserting they are equivalent in spite of the analogies. The focus of this book is *counseling*, in a very broad sense, with clients for whom religious matters are significant. Counseling has been variously defined but here it means the professional utilization of a personal relationship to help a client reach important personal goals, whether or not the client can define them at the start of the work. This is not intended to be a systematic treatment of counseling, available in several books. Instead I want to deal with a number of specific concepts and methods that I think enable the counselor (counselor, social worker, minister, probation worker, therapist) to assist the client explore and resolve their questions or difficulties in living.

Behind all that will be presented here, there are some basic assumptions about people and counseling which I will try to make explicit.

1. Without downplaying the degree to which people's lives and behaviors can be severely distorted, psychopathology is not my focus as such. Rather, I assume *the person functions*

with adaptive intent. The person's behaviors, thoughts, feelings, attitudes, and interests have meaning and the person is always attempting to do sensible and meaningful things *if* the framework in which the person is operating can be understood.

2. Most people can be helped through verbal means, provided that the counselor is aware that language can also prevent action, and that at some point the client may have to act.
3. The relationship between the counselor and client is the most important vehicle of the counseling process. Through a sensitive scrutiny of this interaction the counselor may be able to understand meanings and intents the client cannot put into words. Related to this is careful attention to the counselor's feelings as another communication from the client (and also the counselor).
4. Counseling can be very difficult and frustrating work. We often work without enough of the information we need, progress can be slow, and clients can sometimes work entirely at cross-purposes to their own stated goals. New solutions are thus quite attractive, as they promise to relieve our frustration and aid the client. Homework, problem-solving exercises, and confrontation seem attractive methods. I sometimes think they make the counselor feel something is being done for the client.

For example, after a fairly intense session working on the basis of her fears of closeness, one client said that this was all well and good, but she wanted to change her behavior and just understanding it was not enough. She hinted at needing some homework. At first I felt defensive, as if I had not done enough, until I realized that this was probably a subtle ploy to push away the feeling of closeness that had developed in the session. This is related to point 3, regarding using your feelings as another message from the client. Reflecting back to her my sense of her behavior led to further exploration of her skill at foiling others who tried to become closer to her.

Confrontation, another popular counseling procedure, is often an intense interaction between counselor and client in which much feeling can be expressed. Clients do not need to confront the counselor, but only themselves. Confronting the client means the counselor has failed to enlist the client's self-directed attention. Less can be more.

5. Counselors are often told that rapport and trust are two features of a good counseling relationship, and that it is nearly impossible to counsel effectively without these qualities. My experience is the reverse. When full rapport and trust have been established, the counseling process may well be over.

   For example, in our first session one client was clearly wary and reluctant to disclose very much. I remarked on her suspiciousness and she agreed. I supported her feelings as perfectly appropriate; she did not know me, there was no reason to trust me, and she should watch me very closely. If I did anything that seemed questionable, she should ask. She then disclosed a single session with another counselor, to whom she did not return, who also remarked on these feelings several times, as though the client should trust the counselor. We worked together for several years.

   Well then, how are trust and rapport developed? I find that while it is very important for the counselor to deal directly with overtly expressed doubts or questions, most of the time starting to deal with the concerns the client presents works effectively in beginning to develop rapport and trust. Most clients come for help, not a relationship, which they frequently fear.

6. Finally, about technique, procedure, method, diagnosis, and theory. In the early days of psychoanalysis and vocational counseling, what was frequently presented in expository texts was "how to" and theory. Some analysts or counselors became more enamored of their techniques and theories than the client's progress, leading to poor work. The corrective was expressed in an attack on techniques and methods, leading to extreme assertions such as, "If it feels good, do it." As I see it, technique, procedure, or method refers to the counselor's systematically organized grasp on what the counselor is doing and why, *but* it has to be entirely natural and an integral part of the counselor's response to the client. Otherwise, it becomes artificial, stilted and fake.

Diagnosis is frequently intimidating since most people still view emotional problems as partly or wholly a failure in will, character, or faith. I deal with this, when a diagnosis is necessary, by discussing this directly with clients, offering them the range of relevant diagnoses and asking, perhaps, which one they prefer. This defuses a potentially tense situation. Explaining the possible consequences of using insurance to clients in terms of a later record is, to my mind, ethical.

No theory has been demonstrated to be better than any other in helping people, but counselors do differ in effectiveness. Nevertheless a theory does give counselors ways to think about what they are doing and to find ways out of the difficulties that inevitably arise. A theory also gives the counselor something to think about in the session so he or she can be more quiet and leave space for the client to work in.[1]

Listening

Listening in counseling is an active, difficult process demanding that the counselor violate several professional and social expectations. Most people in our society are trained to not stare, to not ask personal questions and to not know what is hidden in the motives or meanings of others. Further, many clients come with expectations that the counselor will *give* help and advice. Actually, I find that most clients have already received a great deal of advice. Some of it may be quite good and it has not helped. Some of it hasn't even been tried. Our society's dominant value is active striving toward the solution of problems, well expressed in the motto: "Don't just sit there, do something." Thus the client's stated or implied expectations can prod the counselor into "helping" before an adequate awareness of the nuances of the problems has developed.

What then does the counselor do in active listening? I find it useful to ask myself "Why is this person telling me this? Why does he or she want me to know this? What is this person saying about me, about counseling, or about himself or herself?"

For example, one client who was working on her problem with a sparse, unsatisfactory social life, started the session by telling me in some detail about her current ear infection and how medical treatment had failed to slow it down and now she was temporarily deaf in one ear. She apparently changed subjects to tell of an unplanned-for, casual, but entirely innocent date with her roommate's brother who was visiting. The brother was currently unemployed but was on a lower occupational level when he did work, was a recovering alcoholic who had had his driver's license suspended for drunk driving. His first name was the same as mine. It then occurred to me that reporting her partial, temporary deafness was saying that she did not want to hear what she imagined I would say about such a "date." It was actually her mother who had much to say when she was an adolescent. I shared my sense of this with her and many feelings were expressed about her mother's dissatisfaction with the men she dated.

When the client discloses religious issues, listening both to the client and one's own thoughts and feelings intensifies the problem of working with personal values, issues of control, respect for a client's autonomy, and handling symbolically expressed communications.

In an initial consultation with a young woman, she expressed her feeling of being out of place in a religious sense. She was deeply involved with her local Methodist church, with plans to eventually go on for the ministry. Her friends were interested in questions of the Bible's "inerrancy" and "gifts of the spirit," while she was more interested in social justice and related issues. Since Methodism is not rigid in its approach to the Bible and is actively interested in refracting social justice through the prism of faith, it was her friends who were not centered within their tradition. Knowing this about Methodism helped me to hear her own sense of alienation expressed in the guise of a religious problem.

Delineation of the Initial Problem

I recently took my car to the dealer and told the mechanic that I thought the problem was with the starter. When first trying to start it, there was almost no reaction from the starter. Turning the key again got a little more grinding. Turning the key once again got still more grinding and a start. I thought that if the problem was the battery, there would be less and less power each time I activated the starter. As it turned out, the mechanic found the battery needed replacement and that the starter tested out according to "specs." The car has been working well without a return of its symptoms or a new starter. My reasoning was plausible, but I was wrong nevertheless.

Analogously, clients will present their grasp of their problem and this is the place to begin. "One begins where the client is" is an old social work motto. To stop there without reason is an error.

For example, a mother presented herself at a clinic for help with her two sons, aged 6 and 3½. At the initial interview she expressed concern about the effect on both boys of the loss of their father, whom she was divorcing. The interviewer noticed that, as she attempted to inquire about the boys' problems, the mother kept returning to her own concerns. After a short time, the interviewer realized that the mother was deeply burdened and offered the mother someone of her own to talk with to help her with her problems.

If a client begins with a question or problem that has a religious theme, this has to be addressed at the outset. Questions about the counselor have been discussed previously, but another commonly expressed fear is the impact of counseling on the client's faith. The temptation is to reassure clients that their faith will be undisturbed, when at best the counselor can only pledge to not deliberately undermine that faith. To promise to support the client's faith is an expensive commitment, since the counselor cannot tell what this feared danger to the client's faith is about. These are matters to be explored. What is more likely is that behind the question is the client's fear of an attack on someone important to the client. Behind *that* fear probably lies the client's anger, criticism, or distrust of some person, or issues about their faith. This latter is most unlikely to be available at this early point.

Another early issue may be the emotional presence of the client's minister. Whether the minister has referred the client, counseled the client in the past, offered spiritual direction, or discouraged the client from seeking counseling, ministers or lay religious people (nuns, brothers, church youth leaders) are important in the lives of religious clients. If the minister is a positive factor at this point, then his or her impact may not be a matter of immediate concern. When the minister opposes or disapproves of the client's involvement in counseling, this should be dealt with. First one may explore just how this opposition is expressed. It may be the client's own views, or a general remark from the minister. If the pastor clearly disputes counseling, this needs inquiry with the client. If the client freely consents, the counselor may find it useful to contact the clergyman to discuss this reported opposition. Sometimes this is a distortion on the client's part, but where the report is accurate, the minister's fears need exploration and an effort to resolve them. Otherwise the risk of damaging opposition is substantial. See chapter 6 for more detail.

The Social Context

All people live within some sort of community. Isolated people *had* some sort of family, even if they are without current family or friends. Typically most people have families, friends and communities. If the counselor is working with a child brought by one or both parents, not involving the parents in the treatment process in some way increases the likelihood of failure through their not supporting the work of the counselor because of ignorance, fear of change, or premature withdrawal. When working with young unmarried adults, the counselor faces a relatively unencumbered situation, but when a spouse or significant other people exist, the situation is inherently more complex. Taking the position that the counselor just works with the material presented by the client allows one to ignore these outside factors; they do not go away. Most counselors will refuse to accept responsibility that belongs to the client, a position that has received cogent arguments.[2] Not to deal with *any* of the problems that emerge in treatment, except those related to the management of counseling, is much more problematic.

When dangerous suicidal or homicidal impulses, serious acting-out behavior (including spouse abuse, severe anorexia), endangering medical conditions, or sexual and/or physical abuse of a child are present, these are ignored at risk to the client, the treatment, and the counselor. There is a developing body of statute and case law[3] relating to these areas that is changing at a brisk pace. To just apply the usual procedure may be as damaging as not doing anything. Child abuse is universally regarded as very harmful, but not all child abuse situations are equal, a fact usually not recognized in state reporting requirements. Thus, the parent who may be severe in his or her corporal discipline of a child, who recognizes and wishes to change these behaviors and is actively involved in treatment is not distinguished from an abusive, alcoholic parent who is incestuously exploiting his children and is unavailable to treatment. To treat the first parent in the same manner as the second has a significant likelihood of impairing the counseling process.[4] In some jurisdictions, professionals are able to work informally with the Protective Services worker both to satisfy the requirements of the law and to maintain the treatment. Sometimes, the parent may be helped to make a self-report to forestall more destructive interventions. Similarly, tactful and thoughtful exploration of other problematic situations can produce useful progress.

The religious person also operates, in most instances, within a faith community (church, synagogue, mosque). It may be disconcertingly easy to inadvertently blunder into difficulties with the client.

For example, I was working with a young adolescent referred for a suicide attempt. His parents were members of a conservative church that focused on the Book of Revelation. He talked about some of what he had been learning and since his fantasies and artistic productions were gory, I remarked that this book of the Bible was probably a message of support and condolence to some of the Christians of that time who were undergoing painful persecutions. He immediately asked if that meant it wasn't true. Oops!

There are real areas of conflict between the perspectives of most secularly based counselors and some religious denominations. Certain conservative religious and counseling leaders have argued that secular counseling and psychotherapy is devoid of moral values, emphasizes self-centered pleasure-seeking and so on.[5] This is a complex topic, but the values inherent in counseling are quite real even if not immediately manifest.[6] Briefly, one aspect of the counseling process is for the client to grasp and understand his or her own nature, life, and needs. To do so, the client needs to be honest with himself and with the counselor. Honesty is both a basis and a goal of the process. When the counselor is nonjudgmental, the client feels less threat and can better face the problems that prompted the need for counseling. The problem of a skeptical or hostile minister is discussed in the latter part of chapter 5.

Explanation, Interpretation, and Empathy

These terms generate much debate, multiple definitions, and confusion in counseling and psychotherapy. Some theorists reject one or another concept, while others deem one or another as the sovereign remedy that will cure one and all, or is the only activity for the counselor or therapist to engage in. My position is that all have a place and that certainty of the exclusive place of one technique over all others does not befit our current state of knowledge. Having said that, however, it helps to understand how each fits in.

An *explanation* is simply a statement that imparts largely cognitive information in a straightforward fashion. Sometimes this is purely descriptive, as when I explain what my policy is about a client cancelling a session. A more complex, but more typical example is when I explain how I work, and why. I will say something like:

"I am interested in whatever you want to tell me, whatever comes to mind, and whatever dreams you have. Try not to censor what you say. The reason for this is that people's minds were solving problems long before there were counselors. After a problem has been solved by a person, the solution eventually becomes an automatic process, so the person can deal with new problems. If the situation changes, the automatic process doesn't always work well and when that happens, we need to put the solution back into 'manual' mode to develop a new solution. Saying whatever comes to mind helps get around the automatic solutions now in place."

Most clients find this a reasonable explanation and it reduces their initial reluctance to do something they learned was silly: that is, to just talk without having a goal or purpose. We have words for such behavior, such as chatter or babble. A sensible person does not want to do that in front of a stranger, especially a professional stranger.

Explanations can also go further. They can provide information about how things work that only other people can furnish, such as how the world works. Many lower-class clients do not know how to deal with the "system" which is supposed to help them, or how to prepare for a job interview. Explanations can be efficient ways to transmit useful knowledge. There are limits to explanation that will be clearer when we consider interpretation.

Interpretation is a process similar to explanation but designed to help clients see something meaningful about their lives; how past experiences are still affecting them, the effects or meanings of their behaviors, and what events or experiences mean to them emotionally. In a sense, interpretation is an emotional explanation and is intended to create an *insight* in the client. If both feelings and understanding are joined, insight and awareness should be the result. As the sole activity of the counselor, interpretation has definite limits, yet concise, accurate, well-timed interpretation with some clients can be very helpful.

For example, the client previously referred to with the ear infection who had a date with what her mother would have thought an unsuitable man was given an interpretation about her expectation of my reaction to her date. I said "I think you don't want to hear what I think about this date with Bob." I did not explain where I got the material for the interpretation from (her earache), which would have only diluted the effect of my statement. As an interpretation it was concise, related to her feelings, and she supplied the understanding and feelings by going directly to her experiences with her mother's criticisms. Unlike an explanation, which is made in a largely literal form, an interpretation may be allusive, metaphoric, or symbolic in form. An interpretation *connects* or *reconnects* experiences, ideas, feelings. For some, but not all, clients[7] this is very effective where the client already possesses the necessary data but the bridges are missing. Interpretation is not effective where the data are missing, and here explanation may be useful.

There's a negative side to interpretation too. It may be done before the feelings are well enough activated, sometimes cutting off the emotions that need to be present. Then too, interpretation may become an intellectual game that impedes counseling. A more important drawback is that an interpretation implies the counselor knows more than the client. Tactful wording is very important[8] to reduce injury to the client's self-esteem. Interpretations that show how smart the counselor is may not help, while interpretations made to the client that the client could do if invited to, do not foster strength and self-reliance.

Empathy is a much misunderstood word, often taken as close to, or even indistinguishable from sympathy. As used here, a quite different process is intended. Empathy refers to the counselor's effort to experience the client's world from within the client's position.[9] A simple example is the assumption stated at the beginning of this chapter that *a person functions with adaptive intent*. Thus, rather than regard the person's behavior or emotions in terms of degree of pathology, I try to understand the client's aim or intent.

For example, the client with the ear infection whose problems in intimacy were expressed in a lack of a social life had begun to complain about not getting anywhere. (I often found that complaints about lack of progress in counseling, if nurtured, were followed by significant growth.) This woman traveled over 100 miles each way for a lengthy session each week and paid her fee without the aid of insurance, a measure of her considerable investment in the counseling. I had felt for some time that while she was attached to treatment and liked me personally, there was a marked emotional reticence and wariness.

In one session, as we talked over a dream in which she depicted herself as much below her current professional status, she saw this dream as related to therapy. I suggested she felt used, but this was perhaps only partly correct. At the same time it led to my expressing my sense that she wanted something from me but could not ask. In turn, her feeling became clearer that she could not risk asking for what she needed, as it would turn me away. She applied the image of Medusa to herself, remarking that her mother was afraid of snakes and I replied "Medusa turned people to stone; you turned your mother to stone." (Her mother was depressed shortly after her birth because of a second pregnancy only five months later.) I conveyed to her that her fear of expressing what she wanted was her fear she would drive me away.

What made this primarily an empathic rather than an interpretive response was my effort to understand her fear of intimacy as a sensible wish to preserve her good relationship with me, based on the faulty understanding of the toddler who felt her intense emotional needs caused the mother's withdrawal.

Resistance, Transference, and Countertransference

These three concepts arose from Freud's experience with his patients and himself. He labeled it *resistance* when his patients, although in great emotional pain, obstructed the work of psychoanalysis with a variety of behaviors, such as not coming to sessions, not talking, etc. He called it *transference* when the emotional reactions of his patients in analysis strongly resembled emotional patterns established earlier in life, which were transferred to the analyst. *Countertransference* occurred when the analyst, just like the patient, had emotional obstacles that prevented a correct emotional understanding of the patient. Personal analysis was regarded as the remedy for the analyst's transference (i.e., countertransference).

At first resistance and transference were regarded as features of psychoanalysis but they are now understood to be general human qualities. People wish to avoid the anguish of anxiety, shame, guilt, and painful memories if possible (resistance) and they generalize from prior learned experiences (transference).

Some professionals, if they recognize these phenomena at all,[10] view them as irrelevant. Unfortunately resistance and transference do not go away but, if recognized and employed discerningly, can advance the counseling process measurably. When considered, they may illuminate certain past treatment failures too. In brief, where the counselor believes that something within the client is interfering significantly with the counseling process, this needs to be raised; but merely to tell the client that he or she is resisting is accusatory and ineffective.

For example, I saw a man of about fifty who was afflicted by long-standing problems with erectile competence. A serious Catholic, but no longer married, he was troubled by enduring feelings of inadequacy about his sexuality, attractiveness, educational accomplishment, and language competence. After a couple of meetings I asked him to come in with his current girlfriend, who was supportive but also burdened by her own emotional difficulties. I gave them a sensate focusing exercise[11] with directions not to continue to sexual intercourse. At this point, he immediately raised the question of whether this was sinful. His concern did not feel authentic. When we discussed sexual matters in earlier sessions, something similar had happened, but this pattern was now much clearer. With his girlfriend there, I was reluctant to take up the apparent resistance. In the next session he reported two quite successful sexual encounters with his girlfriend. By this point, it was the fourth session and I thought he might be able to use some authoritative information, so I suggested he consult with a member of the pastoral team at a local Catholic church. In the next session he had consulted one of the persons I suggested and found it interesting. He also broke off with his girlfriend, feeling she did not love him enough, and we explored his deep need for total love from his partner. He never returned. In a phone contact, he claimed that child support expenses prevented continued counseling.

I felt this client's resistance was clear enough, but I was diffident about a more direct approach so early in counseling. He seemed an unsophisticated man whose religious feelings obstructed his awareness of his anger at his mother's premature death followed by his early recruitment to work for his father. But his religion was also very important to him. While I cannot be sure, I think I failed to act soon enough on his resistance. His break with his girlfriend reported in the last session was, in retrospect, a warning that I had waited too long.

Two further points need to be made. First, resistance is not usefully overcome by persuasion, appeals to authority, or "willpower." Rather, resistance needs the counselor's respect as a message from the client about something that is bothering the client. This message may be that the material being discussed is painful, or the counselor is on the wrong track, or is out of tune with the client. Frequently the client's major difficulty is wrapped up in the resistive behavior and if the meanings in the resistance can be understood and worked out, the counseling can advance.

Second, the counselor's feeling about the client may be other than just the counselor's personal problems. Sexual feelings in the counselor may reflect the client's wish for closeness, or idealization of the counselor, or effort to test the counselor's trustworthiness, or resistance, or seductive behavior. The therapist's sleepiness or boredom may well indicate the client's emotional detachment. Hostility or anger may signal the client's self-rejection, or frustrated dependency feelings, or fear of closeness, to name a few. Thus the counselor's feelings may well represent important communications about the client's emotional state that he or she cannot articulate. No simple translation is available; rather the counselor must begin to look at the context of the ongoing counseling interchange, what such feelings may have meant in the past, and the counselor's own emotional patterns. The counselor may find consultation with a colleague useful.

The Counselor's Preparation for Work with Religious Clients

The argument as to whether counselors are born or made continues, sterile as ever. The either/or terms of the debate guarantee its futility. There are, however, differences in personal style. Some counselors are demonstrably better than others at connecting with clients, providing a stable, soothing, and supportive environment, making sense of what the client says, selecting the emotionally important issues to respond to, and being heard. No one seems to be born with this skill any more than with the ability to converse.[12] The one clear advantage to the position that counselors are born is that no one has to work to develop the ability.

In addition, the counselor needs a background in current theories in spite of our current limitations in knowledge. Theories give multiple perspectives on a problem, suggesting possible alternatives. Related to theory is an understanding of the counseling process and this is best developed through supervision of actual counseling extended over a considerable period of time. One year of supervised experience is a bare minimum, followed by further supervision in either the training program or a work setting. In addition to a grasp of theories, and a comprehension of the counseling process, there are contents within the various facets of the counseling domain. These may include a knowledge of standard test instruments and vocational families, if these are important to that aspect of counseling the counselor is addressing. A detailed knowledge of the effects of divorce, or substance abuse, or adoption may be important. In all of these, a grasp on what is now known about the complexities of human motivation is presumed to undergird this entire enterprise. It is more pleasant, perhaps, to believe a father's assertion that he has *only* the interests of a child at heart in a custody dispute, but it hardly seems likely. Or a mother who explains her overprotective behavior as *only* a concern to protect her child may really believe that, but the professional should be silently skeptical.

While independent study and on-the-job training have occasionally served for a few individuals, there are real advantages to a coherent program of study and training. In addition to current requirements for certification or licensing, one outcome for the counselor is the formation of a professional identity arising from interaction with (one hopes) respected experts. This identity emotionally sustains the professional at difficult times and suggests modes of problem-solving that are not available through independent study.

There is a temptation to divide the world into clients (who need help) and counselors (who provide help). Identification as a counselor can be a defense if the universal clienthood of all of us is denied. The counselor's obstacles to self-awareness are not inherently different from the client's, and usually benefit from the same remedy. Personal counseling or psychotherapy is an important part of both personal and professional preparation. Most counselors and therapists who have undertaken this uneasy journey esteem it highly as a part of their professional preparation.

Finally, particularly relevant to work with religious clients is a broad-based understanding, both of how religiousness[13] functions within the emotional and cognitive makeup of the client, and of the nature of the various denominations likely to be found in this country. The next section of this chapter attempts to return to many of the denominations discussed in the last chapter, considering how they may sway personality.

Personality Implications of Modern American Religions

When one sees a client for whom religious issues are significant, it is no trick at all to discover that their religiousness parallels important past experiences. This parallel leads to the ready assumption that religion has personal roots that *explain* religion; but this is an overgeneralization. What is explained is the individual form of this person's religiousness, not religion as such, which needs a quite different sort of explanation. Religion is generic to human societies, although individuals vary widely in their degree of religiousness. Explanations of the sources and form of a person's individual religious expression can have important implications for counseling, but there are real limits as to generalizability beyond the individual context.[14] Thus my purpose here is not to outline a psychology of religion but to consider the implications of various denominations for the individual person.

An added dimension, however, is that while there is a dominant value orientation within an ethnic, social or cultural group, there are also variant orientations that give a society a rounded character. The energetic American or thrifty Scot are stereotypes of national qualities with limited use unless one is aware that a society needs a welter of qualities to function effectively.[15]

Judaism

In some ways Judaism is as much a puzzle to its adherents as to non-Jews. Comprising less than three percent of the American population, with about six million Jews, they should have disappeared long ago. Almost invisible in architecture and the visual arts, they are overrepresented among Nobel Prize winners by a nine-fold margin. What could God have been thinking of when he selected this insignificant, nomadic clan to bear his message and be his reluctant witnesses?[16]

Although Jews settled in Ethiopia, India, and China, there were two main geographic divisions among Jews that grew up after the destruction of the Jewish state by the Romans in 70 C.E. The first, centered in the Mediterranean basin were eventually known as the *Sephardim* because of the high and successful culture they developed in Spain. Their vernacular was Ladino, a variant of Spanish. Expelled from Spain in 1492, they experienced a gradual cultural decline as they lived more or less quietly with their Arab and Turkish neighbors. The other main group, known as the *Ashkenazi*, developed in Western Europe. Their vernacular was Yiddish, a variant of fourteenth century German. With the persistent persecutions that characterized their lives, many migrated to Eastern Europe and it was from here that many Jews emigrated to the United States around the turn of this century, eventually outnumbering both their more cultured cousins from Western Europe and the Sephardim who had arrived earlier. It was in Eastern Europe that the *Hasidic* (pious) movement originated; these now comprise a major part of ultraorthodox Jewry. There are three other main divisions in Jewish practice: Orthodox, Conservative, and Reform. *Orthodox* refers to the modern practice of what was traditional Jewish life, and entails strict adherence to dietary, ritual, and ethical practices. The *Reform* movement arose in the early part of the nineteenth century in Germany, as an effort to adapt traditional practices to modern life and the opportunities that were developing as the ghettos in Western Europe were disintegrating. The *Conservative* movement was a counterreaction to the

Reform movement, which many felt had gone too far.

Judaism may be better understood as a culture than as a religion, for the family is the crucible of character formation and socialization to the norms and values of the group. Common joking references to the "Jewish mother" deal with the compelling reality of an active, powerful mother who, even in the traditional family, was usually a determining influence. This is not a modern invention. Proverbs 31:10–31 indicates "the degree of managerial responsibility evidently assumed by the wife of a well-to-do man in ancient Israel."[17] Her emotional importance is also clear in these verses.

The father's role is not eclipsed, but his impact comes to bear somewhat later in the life of the developing child. Boys have certain ritual duties and privileges that make for inequities between men and women, and boys frequently are more esteemed. Only a man can give a legal divorce under Jewish law, but only a Jewish mother can make a person a Jew by birth. Women have very significant roles and functions (beyond childbearing) that give power but not equality in the traditional home. In individual homes the power balance may tilt one way or another.

Industriousness, adult study, educational accomplishment, familial devotion, enjoyment of legitimate pleasures, careful observance of both ritual and ethical practices, and a concern for the needy are traditional values inculcated in the child, through parental behavior, the synagogue and the Jewish school. The implications are manifold. Hard work in the service of the family is valued, but ascetic self-sacrifice is not. Parental "blackmail"—parents using their sacrifices to make demands upon the children—is, however, legendary. Using education to achieve beyond the parents' accomplishments is considered acceptable and is usually supported, while rejection of family values is not.

Joy and satisfaction are religious duties, although an admixture of guilt is to be expected. Sexual satisfaction is expected for men and women but an unmarried man is both pitied and regarded as a "boy." Alcohol use begins very early; wine is a sacramental part of the Sabbath, the Passover observance (four glasses), and certain synagogue festivals. Drunkenness is strongly disapproved of and alcoholism among Jews seems relatively lower than in the general population. Overeating is more likely to be a problem. Because religious activities are centered in the home, religion is not separate from life but saturates and sanctifies it.

This necessarily brief and simplified sketch points to certain outcomes. Jews are more than likely to have difficulties with independence and autonomy vis-à-vis the family, and guilt over efforts in this direction is likely to be strong. Intellectual debate and criticism are not sins but are esteemed even in traditional writings.[18] The self-examination that counseling fosters is entirely compatible with Jewish thought and practice,[19] but may carry with it an obsessive, doubting, or intellectualizing style that can impede the process. The use of medical aid was always esteemed, while relying on God to do for you what you could do for yourself was rejected.

In theory, permissible sexuality is celebrated, but long centuries of persecutory confinement in cramped ghettos led to strong restraints on even the legitimate expression of such needs. Emotional conflicts are frequent in this area. The group cohesion that developed among Jews served to prevent intermarriage, but was, of necessity, capable of strong psychological sanctions. The selection of a partner who is not Jewish indicates the likelihood of significant emotional issues with one or another parent in areas related to intimacy, autonomy, and/or control.

Catholicism

There is a myth not yet dead among some non-Catholics that Catholicism is a monolithic, all-enveloping entity opposed to all that is interesting, intellectual, sexual, or liberal. To begin with, *the* Church is, in reality, several Churches, both in time and location. The rigidity and legalism that characterized the Roman Catholic church after the Council of Trent in the mid-sixteenth century reflected a beleaguered mentality that did not epitomize the Church during the Middle Ages nor in the modern age (from Pius XII and John XXIII).[20] The Eastern church was highly creative in the early development of Christianity, suffering many of the early disputes and schisms. The Great Schism of 1054 that supposedly led to the major division into the Eastern Orthodox church and the Roman Catholic church was actually finalized 150 years later with the sack of Constantinople by the Fourth Crusade.[21] After the conquest of Constantinople in 1453 by the Seljuk Turks, the Eastern Orthodox church gradually retreated into an ossified posture, compared to its earlier creativity. The Russian Orthodox church arose from the Eastern church, took root just before the end of the first millennium, and within a few centuries was established with Moscow as its center.

Though they are not nearly the size of the Roman Catholic church in this country, there is a welter of "other" Catholic churches based on a complex history of growth, competition, schism, and reunion. The Eastern church is much more federated in character without the same authoritative structure as the Roman church; closer both to its Hebraic base and to its mystical roots in thought, liturgy, and ritual, and less burdened by the Western Scholastic tradition. There are differences in theological concepts, the option for a married priesthood (before ordination), certain sacramental practices, and the primacy of the Roman papacy.[22]

In this century the number of adherents worldwide in the Eastern Orthodox church has remained static but the church's percentage of the world population has shrunk to about one-third compared to 1900. Of about 124 million members worldwide, some four million live in the United States, splintered among many groups so that their influence, while perhaps significant in certain places, is not of national magnitude. On the other hand, the Roman Catholic church has nearly tripled in number of adherents, although its "market share" has risen only slightly from 16.8 percent to 18.5 percent throughout the world. In the United States Roman Catholics number over fifty two million,[23] making them the largest Christian denomination. The prejudices and discrimination suffered by Catholics in the last century and the first part of this century have declined greatly, but the parochial system of education developed to protect Catholic children from the proselytizing and erosive effects of public education in the past is still a functional system.

Although few Jews, Roman Catholics, or Eastern Orthodox would appreciate the similarities, there are a number of parallels worth noting. The differences are frequently obvious but all three have a large degree of ritual, an extensive, sung liturgy, a complex body of authoritative tradition, and longstanding practices of study. Elements of church ritual duplicate those of the Jerusalem Temple and the modern synagogue. On a personal level, all three saturate the lives of their adherents, affecting life and death, procreation, and celebration. The implications for personality are profound, but there are major national differences. Irish and Italian Catholics typically show considerable differences with regard to patterns of alcohol use, degree of emotional expressiveness, ease of self-disclosure, and so on.

In general a person of Eastern Orthodox background (perhaps including Eastern-rite or Byzantine Catholics) is likely to be more accepting of pleasure and satisfaction and somewhat less rigid about the minutia of practices than a person with a Roman Catholic background. In addition to important ethnic differences, family differences have powerful individual effects. For many Catholics, guilt and shame are prominent emotions attending many activities related to autonomy, or violation of the precepts inculcated in childhood. Shame and guilt are discussed below in the next section.

When some Roman Catholics talk of their childhood they are likely to relate stories that seem unbelievable to outsiders, such as girls being warned not to wear highly polished or patent leather shoes to avoid reflecting their underwear, or not to accept a dinner date with a young man if a white table cloth is used, as this will suggest a bed sheet and arouse impure thoughts. Boys have been instructed as to the admissible number of times they may compress their penis to expel the remaining urine after urination. This is clearly designed to avoid masturbatory involvement. While some Catholic adults may ridicule such stories, many will confess residual traces of discomfort over one or another specific behavior. Not all Catholic clients have had such experiences, as there is much diversity. I would speculate that the Catholic church in the Midwest is quite a bit different from the Church on the East coast in being less institutionally rigid and more inclined toward social action.

The sacrament of reconciliation (penance) is significantly different between the Eastern and Roman churches. In the Eastern church, the priest aids the penitent in confessing to God (they both face the altar,) while past practice in the Roman church places the priest much more in the role of conduit or intermediary. This has changed considerably since Vatican II but for many clients, confession seems similar to counseling. One problem is that failure to fully confess (just mortal sins)[24] invalidates the efficacy of confession. For counseling however, resistance as a universal phenomenon guarantees that not everything *can* be "confessed" at any one time.

Skepticism toward the therapist's authority, particularly after earlier exposure to pomposity, hypocrisy, or other failings in parents or clergy, including monks and nuns (who are technically laity) is not uncommon. I find it useful to support such feelings and I raise the client's distrust of me. Significant inhibitions are found over (1) bodily pleasure (erectile or orgasmic dysfunction), (2) satisfaction over accomplishment (excess humility), or (3) bodily adornment. Sometimes these problems can arise from a hostile refusal to satisfy someone else, as in the instance of the man with an erectile dysfunction mentioned earlier, but often they represent the deeply ingrained fear of disapproval by important persons in the client's life. It is important to remember that wide cultural differences exist; Catholics of Mediterranean origin are less likely to suffer this sort of problem than are Catholics from northern Europe or the British Isles.

Shame and Guilt

Let us briefly detour to discuss shame and guilt, but not just with regard to Catholicism. Shame seems to develop earlier than guilt in people, and involves an interpersonal relationship. Often the person fears, or has experienced damage to that relationship. Shame (and humiliation, embarrassment, and chagrin) also occurs when the person's integrity or body has been violated (e.g., rape or incest).

Guilt and shame are very important emotions to deal with in counseling, but I find that reassurance is not effective. Guilt is frequently misplaced so that what clients say they feel guilty about appears trivial or incomprehensible. If the problem can be explored in detail, it is frequently possible to find that the client feels guilty about some idea, impulse, or feeling toward another person that, if put into action, would merit guilt feelings. Shame is harder to expunge in counseling and seems to take prolonged work. Sometimes it seems to diminish through this work as if by desensitization, and through the counselor's steady and reliable acceptance. Shame also seems related to repetitively frustrated childhood needs, perhaps followed by ridicule. Subsequently the person has used shame to ward off desires for closeness because that need has become a warning of subsequent hurt and rejection.

Protestantism

One study has indicated that there are over 2,000 Christian denominations in the United States,[25] and most are Protestant. It is not possible to survey all of these, but we will try to consider those that are important in terms of size, and also historical significance. At the risk of oversimplifying, we will consider about two dozen denominations, grouped into nine types of churches: Mainline, Unionist, New Scripture, Millennial, Inner Light, Fundamentalist, Holiness, Pentecostal, and Non-Trinitarian.[26] These groupings are coarse-grained, for all the churches to be discussed differ between each other, and are internally diverse in varying degrees as well.

Mainline Churches

This group comprises the Lutheran, Presbyterian, Reformed, Episcopal, and Methodist denominations. The first three arose at the time of the Protestant Reformation. The Episcopal church came somewhat later, out of Henry VIII's struggle with Rome; the Methodist church was originally a society within the Church of England and did not separate from that church until the end of the eighteenth century.[27]

Worldwide, the Lutheran church is among the largest of the Protestant denominations and has a membership of about eight and one-third million in the United States. The largest group is the Evangelical Lutheran Church of America formed by the recent merger of the American Lutheran Church, the Lutheran Church of America, and the Association of Evangelical Lutheran Churches. This is followed by the Lutheran Church-Missouri Synod and the Wisconsin Evangelical Lutheran Synod, which are progressively smaller and more conservative. The Lutheran and Episcopal churches retain relatively more of their Roman Catholic roots in liturgy, ritual, and sacraments, and are both relatively diverse in degree of sacramental[28] practice, emphasis on biblical literalness, and political liberality.

Perhaps some sense of the kinds of changes and developments that have occurred in the past thirty years may be seen in Table 1, which shows the membership shifts among fourteen denominations or groups of denominations (e.g., Lutherans in Table 1 include American Lutheran Church, Lutheran Church of America, Lutheran Church-Missouri Synod, and the Lutheran Church-Wisconsin Synod). Some denominations, such as Jehovah's Witnesses, show very large percentage changes because the base numbers were small to begin with. Others, such as the Roman Catholics, show a percentage change noticeably smaller than the Southern Baptists, but one that represents more than three times the number of people (nineteen million vs. six million). These data must be interpreted cautiously. Nevertheless, the largest gains have been made among the more conservative churches that tend to offer clear, authoritative answers, while losses of members are seen among some of the mainline (Episcopal, Methodist, Presbyterian/Reformed), unionist (Christian Church/United Church of Christ) and inner light (Church of the Brethren, Mennonite) churches. This latter group, while quite conservative and presenting clear requirements to members, consists of churches that do not actively seek new members.

Among Protestant churches, the Episcopal church, which has been uncharitably characterized as the Republican Party at prayer,[29] is a very diverse denomination, with practices ranging from "high church" or a sacramental level of liturgy that resembles its Roman Catholic origins, to the "broad" or middle church, to a much more austere "low" church with very little of its sacramental structure appearing in its worship services. Far from its Republican

TABLE 1
Changes in Church Membership 1955–1985*

	1955	*1985*	*# Change*	*% Change*
Jehovah's Witnesses	187	730	543	290
Holiness/Pentecostal†	937	3296	2360**	252
Latter-Day Saints	1230	3860	2630	214
Seventh-Day Adventist	277	652	375	135
Salvation Army	250	428	178	71
Southern Baptist	8467	14477	6010	71
Roman Catholic	33397	52655	19258	58
Lutheran	5965	8274	2309	39
Episcopal	2853	2739	−114	−04
Methodist	10030	9267	−763	−08
Presbyterian/Reformed	4021	3391	−631**	−16
Church of Brethren	196	159	−36**	−19
Christian Ch./United Ch. Christ	4014	2800	−1214	−30
Mennonite Church	70	43	−27	−39

(Figures are in thousands of members.)

*Adapted from *Yearbook of American & Canadian Churches 1987* by Constant H. Jacquet, Jr. Copyright © 1987 The National Council of The Churches of Christ in the USA. Used by permission of the publisher Abingdon Press.

†Composed of the Assemblies of God, the Church of God (Anderson, Ind.), and the Church of God (Cleveland, Tenn.). These numbers do not reflect the very large number of Holiness and Pentecostal churches, many of which do not provide statistics to any reporting body. The churches selected were those of larger Pentecostal and Holiness churches that did provide statistics to give a representative picture of changes over time.

**Slight differences due to rounding errors.

characterization, some parts of the Episcopal church are evangelical in vitality and in recruiting others, while other parts of the church are active in attempting to bring about political or social improvement. It is an error to presume that these two modes of activity are mutually exclusive. Episcopalians are not as intense about the role of religion in their lives as are some other denominations, as may be seen in Table 2 (p. 80).

As with all statistics, these require both interpretation and caution. One might conclude that Southern Baptists are much more religious than Episcopalians (74 percent vs. 42 percent rating as Very Important), or that nearly equal numbers of Southern Baptists and Episcopalians see their religion as important in their lives (95 percent vs. 87 percent), or that Episcopalians are more well-rounded and less fanatical in their interests than Baptists. The warning about "lies, damn lies, and statistics" applies here as elsewhere.

The Presbyterian and Reformed churches will be considered together, since both arise from the theology of John Calvin, a French thinker mostly active in Geneva. He was one of a group of theologians who, shortly after Luther's initiation of the Protestant Reformation, developed a series of concepts that were even more radical than Luther's position that faith (in Jesus) alone justified (relieved of original sin[30]) the person. Calvin held that humans were incapable of doing anything to change their state and that only God could choose who would be saved. Such salvation was irresistible.[31] This very condensed sketch would suggest a harsh theology in these churches if the founding theology were still applied. This is not really currently true, any more than reading Luther and Melanchthon brings one up to date on modern Lutheran thought. The diverse denominations under the Presbyterian and Reformed umbrella have certain characteristic similarities; primarily a presbyterian (eldership) governance structure, some retention of sacraments (baptism and communion), and only moderate pressure for doctrinal uniformity. The churches in this group are quite diverse, ranging from liberal to conservative, both theologically and with regard to social action vs. evangelical activity.

Like many denominations, the name Methodist began as a derogatory epithet applied to John Wesley and his college peers for their methodical approach to holiness. Holiness is a specific term referring to a state of spiritual development beyond justification called perfection, or sanctification (freedom from deliberate sin). Wesley, an Anglican priest, never intended to found another church, but only to revitalize his church. His followers only separated from the Church of England after his death. Although Methodists have a reputation for opposing a number of gratifying activities (alcohol, and sometimes dancing, and movies), this has much modified in the United Methodist church in recent times. Methodists are likely to be serious about their faith, but genial in practice,

TABLE 2
Importance of Religion for Selected Denominations*

	Very Important	*Fairly Important*	*Not Very Important*
Southern Baptists	74%	21%	4%
Mormons	71	24	5
Lutherans	55	35	9
Catholics	54	35	10
Methodists	53	37	10
Presbyterians	46	43	11
Episcopalians	42	45	12

*From *Yearbook of American & Canadian Churches 1987* by Constant H. Jacquet, Jr. Copyright © 1987 The National Council of The Churches of Christ in the USA. Used by permission of the publisher Abingdon Press.

without an excessive emphasis on doctrinal minutia or scholarly activity. Social action is an important vehicle for the expression of faith.

Unionist Churches

There are three denominations grouped here: the Disciples of Christ (Christian Church), Churches of Christ and the United Church of Christ. Their beginnings can be traced to Jan Hus a century before the Reformation but in many ways they appear to be an American phenomenon. They developed primarily on the frontier, animated by the desire to have a Christian church not riven by creeds or dominated by hierarchies. They are earnest churches, moderately diverse in theology, though tending toward the conservative end of the spectrum. Next to the Mennonite church, they have shown the largest percentage decline in membership (see Table 1) in the past thirty years. Descriptively, they seem similar to the Presbyterian and Reformed churches, except they do not have the same level of creedal formation.

New Scripture Churches

Most Christian denominations have additional literature that amplifies and expands the core Scripture. Judaism has a similar body of writings in the Talmud and Responsa texts. These sorts of writings are venerated but may not be quite on a par with the Bible, although practically they may be decisive on many issues. The Church of Jesus Christ of Latter-Day Saints (Mormon) and the Christian Science church both have scriptures of a status on a par with the Bible.[32]

To outsiders, both churches have distinctive, even bizarre-appearing characteristics which, while attention-getting, entirely miss the significant emotional qualities of each denomination. Polygamy (Mormon), which has long since been stopped, or faith healing and the rejection of medicine (Christian Science), which stereotype these denominations are not issues central to their faith.

In the Mormon church, people are seen as developing toward a material perfection of their lives in a way to acquire joy and gladness. Service, missionary endeavors, and social welfare activities are expected, at least at some time in everyone's life. Relationships are very important both within and outside the family, but there are very strong barriers against premarital and extramarital sexual activity. Celibacy is strongly disapproved of, particularly in men in this very family-oriented denomination. Alcohol, tobacco, and caffeine are prohibited but some use occurs, at least among college-age students.

The pattern of Mormon life, emphasizing a loving, beneficent God, which is concretely realized in a supportive environment developed within each Mormon community, and is put into effect through expectations of worthwhile, productive activities, makes this an attractive environment. On the more problematic side, there are strong expectations placed upon both children and adults. If alcohol or tobacco is used, there is no "backstop" within the social system once temperance is breached. Autonomy issues and conflicts over control are likely, especially where the person's life trajectory or wishes exceed the permissible boundaries.

Christian Science, which has adopted Mary Baker Eddy's writings as being on the same level as Scripture, could hardly be more different from the Latter-Day Saints. In contrast to the emphasis on the material (i.e., sense-based) character of life in the Mormon church, Christian Science holds that evil is a false perception and illness is attributable to incorrect thinking. So a trained Christian Science healer can, with proper thinking and prayer, induce healing. This is not incompatible with use of meditation and imagery as an auxiliary treatment for cancer, and with fairly well-substantiated data on the relationship between survival rates for breast cancer, psychotherapy, and personality characteristics.[33] Setting broken bones and assistance at birth is permissible. Although numbers of members are not supposed to be reported, it seems that membership in 1989 is below 170,000 compared to 270,000 just before the Second World War.[34]

With its strong emphasis on thought, meditation, and imagery, there is a propensity for withdrawal in interpersonal relations, and this is consistent with the treatment of two people from Christian Science backgrounds that I am acquainted with. Both reported parents whose emotional connection with their children was poor.

Millennial Churches

The Seventh-Day Adventists and Jehovah's Witnesses are included here, as both are deeply rooted in the apocalyptic or revelatory imagery of the Book of Revelation, although they are not the only churches which are. The term *millennial* refers to a group of ideas around the thousand-year period described in Revelation, after which a great struggle between Jesus and Satan will end with Satan's defeat and various fates for the faithful and for sinners. The Adventists also have a sizable body of new scripture in the writings of Ellen White, and could have been included in the grouping above. They were placed here both because of the strong millennial emphasis of their theology and because Charles Russell, who founded the Jehovah's Witnesses, was heavily influenced by Adventist thinking.

Adventist theology contains world-destroying imagery, but in practice there is a good deal of emphasis on social service, education, and practical achievement. Many schools at all levels and a large number of medical facilities are supported by the Adventists. Their observance of the Sabbath on Saturday and avoidance of meat not slaughtered in a manner consistent with biblical practices (kosher meat fulfills their needs) did not arouse the ire of their neighbors. Although their theology has a somber tone, with an emphasis on the ever-present danger of giving in to evil, in practice there is a fairly cheerful overall quality. They do not see experiencing temptation as a sin, but giving in to it is, so sin is regarded as a choice. Accomplishment and the satisfactions that go with it are supported, and it is expected that hard work will lead to success.

I have not worked with any Adventist clients but I think they would be vulnerable to anxious concern about making errors and falling prey to evil from which they could not extract themselves in time. In more troubled clients, one might find images of the world being devastated. Such apocalyptic images are not without some foundation in view of the arms race. As a prominent feature of a client's experienced world, I would look for intense, repressed anger and consider the possibility of a history of abuse in childhood or early, severe neglect.

Jehovah's Witnesses have shown the most rapid proportional growth in the past thirty years of all those in Table 1 even though their reported membership was just under three-quarters of a million in 1985. The Witnesses hold that many of the world's ills are attributable to the government, religion, and commercial business. They believe the Papacy has deliberately mistranslated the Bible. Like the Adventists, their view of the world is of a cataclysmic struggle between evil and good. Only a few will be saved, although there seem to be several classes who will be rescued in varying ways from the oncoming catastrophe. Once a group with an extreme imagery and an aggressive proselytizing posture, they evoked strong hostile reactions from those who found their doctrines unacceptable. Their missionary activity is no longer aggressive, but it is still vigorous. This denomination is sometimes characterized as more pathological than most others,[35] but the evidence is anecdotal. The elders who direct each Kingdom Hall (they reject "churches") are reputedly unfavorable to psychotherapy.

Inner Light

There are a number of small but historically important churches in this group: Amish, Church of the Brethren, Mennonite church, and The Society of Friends (Quakers). The Quakers are currently important through their humanitarian and social welfare activities. None are active proselytizers, and the first three seem to discourage new members. The Church of the Brethren and the Mennonite church both report dramatic membership losses over the past thirty years and presumably the Amish have also suffered losses, but not all churches report statistics. The Quakers are composed of several groups, some of which resemble other Christian churches with organized worship services, and some which conduct the silent services the Quakers are known for.

The Inner Light category refers to a concept of openness in experience to an inner light from God, and particularly characterizes the silent Quaker services. All the churches in this group share a specialized and decorous mysticism called "enthusiasm"[36] in which the goal is closeness to God in order to hear His message. This is not delusional or hallucinatory, but is a particular expression of spirituality. Community is quite important in these churches. This is especially true of the inward-turning nature of the Amish and Mennonite churches. The stress on service for some Quaker churches is consistent with their community emphasis. The quiet and decorous behavior of people in these churches may obscure their passionate attachment to their way of life. Emotional difficulties are likely to center about guilt or shame over not meeting community standards. Feelings of failure and disloyalty may trouble a member who has abandoned the community through advanced learning, improved socioeconomic status, or not following the community's practices and observances.

Fundamentalist, Holiness, and Pentecostal

To many people these three terms seem interchangeable, but they are not. To add to the confusion, evangelical and charismatic are two related but distinct terms that are frequently grouped here. Other than noting the diversity seen in these churches, and that they tend to be theologically conservative, it is hard to generalize about people in these churches. Many, but not all, Baptist churches can be included here. Those unfamiliar with the Baptist movement may equate Baptist with Southern Baptist, which is an error. Some northern and general American Baptist churches are much more centrist in thought, and in principle Baptists have rejected political involvement.

Fundamentalism is a relatively new concept that characterizes a movement that began in the United States at about the start of this century. Fundamentalism arose in reaction to the changes in traditional Protestant Christian thought and practices introduced by liberal pastors and theologians. It represented an adherence to certain "fundamental" principles, including a belief that the Bible is to be taken as written (literally), for it is without error (inerrancy), a belief in the Trinity, and in the substitutionary death of Jesus. Most other Christians see His death as atoning too, but not as a punishment for His sins. Some fundamentalists take literalism literally; that whatever is written in the translation they are attached to (frequently the King James Version) is the final word. Others take literalism to refer to the original text, recognizing that the received text of the Bible has been damaged to some degree. Typically, fundamentalist worship is relatively restrained. Bible study and reliance on biblical texts is very important, while intense emotional displays, such as speaking in tongues (glossolalia) is frowned upon. Currently many Fundamentalists are actively trying to suppress the teaching of evolution, or failing that, to provide instructional time for a Creationist view of the world. This matter also arouses many who are not technically fundamentalists but who accept the principle of biblical inerrancy.[37]

Holiness (or Perfectionism) began as a society within the Methodist church, just as Methodism began within the Church of England. As was mentioned earlier, holiness or perfection sprang from Wesley's concept of entire sanctification, where it was viewed as a gradual process. In Holiness circles it is regarded as something that could happen through a brief, intense change. Holiness churches do not typically approve of speaking in tongues. Although many religious movements began in Europe, the Holiness movement made a reverse Atlantic crossing, having a significant effect on the Englishman William Booth, founder of the Salvation Army. Then it returned to the United States where the Salvation Army has enjoyed a growth of over seventy percent in the past thirty years.

Pentecostalism originated from the Holiness movement, and went beyond the "second blessing" of holiness to the "third blessing" of baptism in the Holy Spirit. This was characterized by "gifts of the Spirit," such as speaking in tongues which is described in Acts 19:6.[38] A number of other "gifts" are described in I Corinthians 12:4–11, including teaching, leading and healing. Some Pentecostal churches may use Holiness in their name but few Holiness churches will use Pentecostal. Pentecostal churches are prone to schism. There are many of them, and they tend to affiliate only in relatively loose associations.

Evangelical derives from a Greek word meaning "good news" and refers to the Christian impetus to give others the good news of the atoning death and resurrection of Jesus. This term also refers to the desire to bring others into communion with Jesus and other Christians to receive salvation. Thus evangelical can refer to activity by anyone without regard to a particular point of view. As typically practiced, evangelically oriented people are also likely to be of a fundamentalist, conservative, holiness, or pentecostal persuasion.

Charismatic is derived from the Greek "charis" meaning grace. The current meanings frequently include connotations of charm, suppleness, or physical skill, but the original meanings had to do with favor or gift (from a powerful personage). In the Bible this frequently meant God. As practiced this refers to expression of intense emotion at points in a service. Charismatic is more likely to refer to a Catholic group than to a Protestant group, where Pentecostal is the more accustomed term.

Non-Trinitarian

This includes two extreme churches, "Oneness" Pentecostal churches and the Unitarian Universalist Association. The former see Jesus as God or Lord and reject the Trinity. They are likely to resent being classed with the Unitarians who are often not regarded as Christian at all. Although not very large (about 172,000), Unitarians represent an ancient and influential line of thought. Goodness and improvement are seen as a human potential, but Unitarians are non-creedal. Some Unitarians might regard themselves as rigidly nondogmatic. Members differ in important ways from most Christian denominations.

Islam

It is a common belief that the United States is hospitable to new religions, as exemplified in the constitutional separation of church and state, but our history is not consistent with this assumption. Most of the new religions that arose in the nineteenth century were ridiculed, and many were persecuted.[39] Islam may be under somewhat less stress today in this country than it would have been in the past because of generally greater tolerance, as well as better control of social disorder. However Islam may also be harassed, in part because of its association with Middle East terrorism. Worldwide Islam has shown an expansion of over 260 percent, and only atheism has shown more growth.[40]

Islam clearly rejects color consciousness and holds forth an attractive, modest life to its adherents. For this and other reasons, it is an attractive faith for blacks in this country who wish to reject any connection with religions associated with whites. There have been other black separatist movements, but the first to have some association with Islam was begun in 1913 by Noble Drew Ali (born Timothy Drew) as the Moorish Holy Temple of Science. Influenced by Islam, but with variants of its own, it fragmented on its founder's death in 1927.[41] Next came the Nation of Islam, started by W. D. Fard about 1931. Fard disappeared in 1934 and leadership devolved on Elijah Poole, who changed his name to Elijah Muhammad. Emphasizing self-improvement, economic independence, hard work, moral behavior, and self-reclamation, while rejecting white society for all the injuries blacks have suffered made the Nation of Islam very effective in fostering a sense of pride and integrity in black people. Elijah Muhammad's message found fertile ground among jailed black men. One of them Malcolm Little (Malcolm X), became an outstanding exponent of that message. Malcolm X was assassinated in 1965, with his murder variously attributed to the Nation of Islam, the New York City Police Department, or the FBI.

When Elijah Muhammad died in 1975, one of his sons (Wallace Deen Muhammad) succeeded him and startled his followers by proclaiming that whites were no longer devils, and began to direct the movement into a much more orthodox and tolerant position with regard to Islamic teachings. As a signal of these revisions he changed the movement's name to American Muslim Mission, and the organization was subsequently accepted by the World Muslim Council. Not all members followed these changes; Louis Farrakhan (born Louis Walcott) reconstituted the Nation of Islam, holding to the separatist doctrines promulgated by Elijah Muhammad.

The image of Islam, formed primarily from the current visibility of several Arab nations and Iran (which is not Arab), may not tell one much about an American-born member of the American Muslim Mission. The Mission's core teachings emphasize thrift, morality, modesty, and integrity. Other factors, individual to the person's family of origin, are also of importance and will need to be understood during the course of the counseling process.

3

Religious Themes in the Life of the Person

The Personal Meanings of Religion

In the previous two chapters, we have looked at religious themes from the perspective of the counselor, the counseling process, and that of specific religious denominations. It is now time to consider religious themes as they function within the life of the person.

Developmental Influences

There are several approaches to understanding religion in the person's life and existence, three of which are common in counseling. The first sees religion largely or wholly in terms of pathology.[1] The second approach treats religion as wholly sacred and not open to significant scrutiny. The third makes it the centerpiece of the treatment process.[2] A fourth approach regards religion in the life of the person as affected by the course of individual development, formed by available cultural and political modes of expression, steered by cognitive and emotional imperatives, leavened by human creativity, expressing noble and base motives,[3] and depicting profound individual experiences in a cosmic idiom. This is the approach taken here.

In varying degrees, all religions value and employ emotionality. Much of the liturgy, from a simple Quaker meeting to a Roman Catholic High Mass, sets an emotional state in the congregant. The liturgy employs words, ideas, and verbal images to communicate thoughts and evoke attitudes. As Pruyser pithily summarized it, "In Catholicism, worship is drama; in Puritanism, it is obedient hearing."[4] Most denominations have an educational arm active through both the institution (church, synagogue, or mosque) and the home. Several influences affect the pattern of religious identification, including cognitive development as a function of age, socioeconomic status, denomination, and features specific to both the child and the family.[5]

Ideally, the denomination should aim its instruction and liturgy at a level fitting the congregant's level of understanding and emotional maturity. Often this is a daunting task. Some clients can recount experiences that promoted growth, altruism, and personal development. Others relate incidents ranging from harshly punitive, to mind-numbing, to grossly violative of their integrity and of the law. Adults (and sometimes child clients) will tell of past episodes of spankings or ridicule by religious teachers or clergy, or threats of awful fates in Hell, or memorizing meaningless syllables in another language (Hebrew or Latin), or regurgitating, under compulsion, exact answers to complex theological questions they cannot begin to grasp.

Often the material presented to children will greatly exceed their capacity to understand, or will be of such simplicity as to induce mind-deadening boredom. Difficult or embarrassing questions may be bypassed, or the child will be told that such questions are not permissible, and even a sin. Hypocrisy or indifference by parents or clergy play their part in convincing the child that this is all a charade. Worst of all, some adults will recall sexual seduction or worse by clergy or ancillary lay workers. One adult related how, as a thirteen-year-old distressed over her parents' divorce, she was seduced by a minister who offered to teach her how to "love" so the same fate would not befall her. Her distrust of authority was not hard to fathom. A counselor may be tempted to assure the client of his trustworthiness in response to such an account. I find treatment goes much better when I support the distrust by clients as a sensible response to their experience.

The client may be alienated for these or other reasons. But if not, even then, various influences act to separate children from their denominations for a time. In our society the developmental thrust is for children to differentiate from their parents. Sometimes this transition passes almost unnoticed, but usually this passage entails an apparent rejection of parental values. Religion is an excellent target. Religious parents may find children who overtly or covertly declare themselves nonbelievers or nonobservers. Nonreligious parents are sometimes similarly surprised to find their child has been "saved" or has become a diligent keeper of practices to which the parents have given only lip service. Often, if the parents do not react too strongly, continue to show their love and acceptance and avoid provocations, the values, beliefs, and practices their children eventually develop will appear little different from those of the parents. But the young adult looking back on religious training may feel that religion is childish. Indeed it is, *if* the person stopped learning about religion at about twelve to fourteen, just when the capacity for true abstract thought has begun.[6]

Cognitive Aspects

Most definitions of religion emphasize beliefs and rituals in varying proportions, but beliefs contain ideas and these are matters people readily disagree about. When belief[7] is prominent in a religion, implanting the religion's doctrines and teachings requires a major effort. Inoculating the recipient against those doctrines that are threatening and held to be false is often equally important.

Frequently a religion's beliefs involve events that confer authority on the world-view these tenets express, and define the status and functions of the members of the community. These authorizing events often are narrated as history, accompanied by signs[8] or revelations, but they come in a form vulnerable to attack as incompatible with current scientific or historical knowledge. It is important to realize that biblical history was not written as objective narrative but to convey ideas about God, humanity, and their mutual relationship. Truth may have meant something partly different from modern concepts, but disinformation and "spin control" are not biblical inventions. Thus the Bible combines objective history, propaganda,[9] natural history, philosophical debate (in story form), and a view of the world quite different from ours. In Exodus, Moses contends with Pharaoh and turns the Nile into blood in which fish die. Modern explanations may suggest that it did not happen, or it was a parable, or that the color was induced by a deposit of red dust from a sandstorm, or from iron oxide leached into the river, and so on. These explanations miss the point. The people in the Bible knew quite well about the seasons and other natural phenomena; their lives depended on knowing these things. Many biblical signs or wonders are clearly described as natural events; what was important was not that some natural event occurred, but that it happened *at that time*—it *meant* something! We will return to this late in this chapter when we discuss miracles.

For the child or adult, now two to four thousand years from these events, having an outlook that offers a radically different view of nature, to insist on the historical truth of these miracles or revelations as a basis for belief is to look through the wrong end of the telescope. We are persuaded by our experience. It is not for nothing that Missouri's auto licenses proclaim it to be the "Show Me" state. To try to persuade others to beliefs through ancient accounts is often ineffective. Beliefs are not only ideas, but also have an emotional component formed through experienced relationships with other *people.* If a religion "works" for a person, it does so most effectively through an identification with someone important to the person, and not because of an ancient story. It is that positive emotional relationship which most effectively authorizes the "truth" of the narrative or miracle. Thus belief is not primarily a matter of theology but one of trust, i.e., group cohesion and individual identity.

When a child or adolescent asks questions or challenges a religious teacher or minister on some point of doctrine or aspect of biblical narrative, several motives may be at work. The youngster may be saying that he or she feels disconnected from the continuing process, or that what is presented lacks credibility in a modern sense, or that he or she may be working out a developmental issue in which increased separation from his or her family or peers is temporarily important, or that he or she dislikes the teacher or pastor, or . . . . When these challenges are handled clumsily or youngsters are made to feel that to ask questions is a sin or lack of faith, then the opportunity for youngsters to enhance their relationship with adults is lost or diminished. Some children suppress their curiosity, their self-esteem ebbs, and they become like the adults whose insensitivity they will transmit to the next generation. Others become alienated and equate the adult teacher's lack of tact with the "falsity" of their religion. In counseling, the anger of these clients needs to be understood not as a mature appraisal of the complexities of their own theology but as a response to disappointment and hurt. One client reported family prayer sessions that prayed for another member to be able to stay on her diet, but for my client's devils to be driven out. This was a devastating message. In that sense, counseling that attempts to directly "repair" the client's faith is at risk to produce greater basic alienation even if counseling achieves apparent success.

The ordinary categories of thought are seen throughout the range of religious ideation. Of these, five will be mentioned: abstraction, concreteness, syncretism, symbolism, and metaphor. *Abstraction* involves a shift in level of description or categorization.[10] Individual items are grouped according to common features into a larger class and this permits more efficient memory storage and reasoning through seeing relations. Abstraction inescapably involves some detachment from direct experience. An orange and a banana each have individual qualities of color, texture, smell, taste, weight, etc. "Fruit" has a much diminished sensory aspect. Abstractions can aid reasoning and memory, or they can block direct experiences, wishes, and feelings. Thus the client who construes events and experiences in very abstract terms is probably avoiding unpleasant thoughts or feelings. When the abstraction has a religious coloration the counselor may wonder if something important is being avoided. "God is Love" is one such abstraction, equating two very complex concepts in such a way that each might mean anything.

Concreteness reverses abstraction, providing direct experiential contact; yet when used to an extreme degree, it serves to avoid meanings, implications, or anxiety. Fundamentalism may be such a form of concreteness,[11] in which the Bible becomes a tangible thing, even an idol, to be taken literally. Some will extend science, which is only a method for understanding and exploring the world, into a concrete set of prescriptions for living.[12] All religions contain complex issues which, at their boundaries, are likely to clash.[13] A persistently concrete approach is one way to avoid recognizing these boundary clashes. Persistent concreteness in a client when more flexibility would be adaptive suggests a problem area, as does insistence on a unique interpretation of a Bible statement or religious practice.

Syncretism is an extension of the abstract attitude but uses such overarching inclusiveness that it is "too trite to be false and too meaningless to be correct."[14] In religious terms, this typically entails the bringing together of disparate, even discordant traditions and ideas. One such example is the "Jews for Jesus" movement. The surface plausibility of the movement relies on Jesus' Jewishness, the overlap between the Old Testament (for Christians) and the Bible (for Jews),[15] and several other similarities in ritual and concept, and glides over decisive differences.[16] As in other areas, the counselor has to differentiate between a creative synthesis and an interest that primarily masks emotional difficulties needing resolution. Indicators that distinguish between creativity and emotional difficulties include:

1. the degree to which the client can articulate conceptual and practical problems in his or her thinking,
2. the internal logical structure of the client's ideas,
3. the client's propensity to brush aside objections and obstacles,
4. the use of simple, banal, and convenient images, and
5. the degree to which the proposed synthesis meets uniquely personal needs.

Symbolism and *Metaphor* are related and partly overlapping. A symbol is some sign that stands for an operation or concept. Thus + means addition, and ' usually means possession when at the end of a word followed by an "s." These are simple symbols. A cross † or a schematic representation of a fish have come to be symbols of two complex, significant aspects of Christianity. Metaphor is verbal, transferring an image from one place to another, and creating new language in the process. Thus, "twilight of the gods" connects ending (of a day) with deities disappearing. The image of God as shepherd is another metaphor. Symbols and metaphor may be very powerful in thinking through problems, distilling complex ideas into compact forms, creating new language to express ideas only partly formed, or communicating with and influencing other people. Symbol and metaphor also seductively invite their own substitution for refractory reality (a metaphoric sentence), sometimes leading to behavior that would otherwise be hard to justify or accept. *Heathen* (from heath or rural area) and *infidel* (from the Latin meaning unfaithful) are more negative than *country cousin* or *member of another faith.*

Language Functions

Symbol and metaphor connect with language in religions. In the three religions here, the *Word* and the *Book* are of central importance. God spoke and the world was created. Adam *named* the animals, Jacob's *name* was changed to Israel and he became different, in the beginning was the Word. What and how we think is highly dependent on the language we have. Thus, the Bible does not apparently discuss *issues*; only stories are told or law declared in the Old Testament. With difficulty, the Hebrew narrators did discuss issues, by using stories. For example, the Book of Ruth tells of Naomi and her two sons Mahlon and Chilion who marry Moabite women, Ruth and Orpah. How was this story heard?

Mahlon and Chilion mean Sickness and Wasting (names no parent would give), while Orpah means She Turns Away (which she does early in the story), so the readers probably understood that this was an allegory. Moab was an enemy country at the time the story was written. The narrative recounts how Ruth, a woman from Moab, becomes the grandmother of King David, who established the kingdom of Israel. The story was set down after the return from the Babylonian exile and makes sense as a political tract, arguing against the practice then being advocated for Jewish men to divorce the non-Jewish wives acquired during the exile. This explanation does not exclude other meanings, but points to the need for care in understanding religious language.

The power of language extends beyond its use as a vehicle for direct expression. Latin, Hebrew, Greek, and other languages may not be comprehensible to the congregant and yet contain emotional meanings not easily put into words. Religious phrases such as "Hallelujah" (literally "praise the Lord (Yah)"), or "Amen" (the biblical equivalent of "right on"), often have more emotion in the original language. In listening to a client who uses language with religious overtones, it is important to note that such language may connect the client with an outside power, a sense of goodness, or superiority, or alignment with important people of childhood. Tactful inquiry may clarify this.

Although religion tends to be separated from sexuality in the minds of most people, some religious language is erotic to a greater or lesser degree. It may have a pious, prophetic, or exhorting overlay, but there are numerous places in the Bible where erotic language appears. When a client employs language with erotic overtones it likely contains erotic feelings the person cannot accept in any direct fashion. Similarly, there are many parts of Scripture that contain accounts of war, violent and extravagant imagery,[17] God's punishment of sinners, and advice on living and to parents (in the Wisdom[18] literature). A particular interest or concern for these kinds of language images, while couched as concern for the child, the future of humanity, or otherwise justified, nonetheless merits exploration in counseling.

Prayer is almost always expressed in a language form. A common understanding of prayer is that one who prays asks for something. While this may be true as far as it goes, prayer can well be confession as a step toward reconciliation with God, adoration or communion with God, or it may have a self-instructional aim. All denominations reject prayer that is insincere, yet the inherent nature of worship invests language with both sacred and ritual qualities. The accretion of a ritual aspect to prayer can lead to the loss of its spontaneous, emotional character, which can destroy the most significant aspect of prayer.

Some clients may ask a counselor to pray with them, or some counselors may offer this. This is a highly personal matter and counselors should not do so even if asked, if they are uncomfortable. The risk of being seen as insincere is high. Where the counselor does not find this uncomfortable, then exploration of the client's intent is indicated. What is being prayed for? Such a request may be an effort to achieve closeness, to secure comfort from a ritual activity, to partake of the counselor's greater "power," to divert attention from a problem area, or to test the counselor's attitudes or sincerity.

Emotion

Religious life values emotion, albeit with differing emphases, depending on the denominational custom, while thinking is sometimes suspect. Not all emotions are equally valued, nor do all religions value the same feelings. Thought and scholarly study are significant facets of certain religions and specific denominations. Roman Catholicism has a long history of scholastic endeavor. The monasteries preserved much of the Greek learning from destruction, yet before the Reformation there were marked restrictions on who could read the Bible. This has slowly disappeared. Other mainline Protestant denominations accept scholarship, although some are more active than others. Protestant denominations not in the mainstream are more varied, though all, or nearly all, value Bible study. Among Jews, study and prayer are nearly equivalent and since Judaism is centered mainly on behavior rather than belief, widely divergent opinions are tolerated.

Pruyser[19] lists seven categories of feelings: longing, reverence, humility, gratitude, compassion (mercy), contrition, and aspiration (zeal), although he notes other lists as well. Other emotions belong here, including awe, dread, love, and bliss. Elsewhere, Pruyser[20] points out that religion (and sometimes art) also contains two other qualities; mystery and transcendence. He discusses these emotions vis-à-vis Christianity, but Judaism would also add intense concentration.[21]

None of these lists include humor, an emotion more likely associated with irreverence. The white-faced clown seems to have originated in medieval Catholic worship as the "holy interrupter." There is a good deal of wordplay in the Bible among the people whose doings are chronicled. Since thoughts or feelings are rarely described, humor has to be inferred, but there is occasionally a sarcastic quality to God's statements. To catch these, look at a translation that translates the Bible literally even though the reading is often wooden.[22]

In brief then, religion operates through the same human processes as any other domain in human existence. Anger, hate, love, eroticism, joy, serenity, kindness, sorrow, remorse, awe, dread, holiness, humor—the list is nearly endless. Perhaps the difference is that in the realm of religion, thoughts develop in the most diverse forms and emotions occur over the widest range of intensity. Few other human activities have more diversity about what is acceptable and what is forbidden.

Control, Regulation, and Revolution

Religions are frequently characterized as control devices in human existence, devised by the aristocracy to rule the mass of peasants. It has long been recognized that religion, employed by sophisticated rulers in certain societies, could exert a governing function.[23] To assume that such control is the *purpose* of religion confuses operation with intent. Religions also exist in many societies where social control is exercised through other means. Religions also *change* societies,[24] and all of the religions considered here began in opposition to the established order.

Another popular explanation of religion is that it arose from magic, and magic is an early technology for controlling the environment. This is superficially appealing, flattering the modern person surrounded by scientific thought and advanced technology. However, anthropological studies[25] show that "magical" practices primarily symbolize experience. Fertility rituals are practiced in the spring, not in winter.

So far religion has not really been defined in this book, but now may be the time to offer a partial definition.[26] Whatever other functions they serve, *religions provide order and meaning to the physical and psychological world.* In general terms, religion is a *meaning-system.* Put this way, we can ask what functions meaning-systems serve. There are several points to be made here.

First, the human nervous system requires external stimulation.[27] If it is not to cause disruption, sensory stimulation requires organizing structures, which are provided by meaning-systems in the human mind.[28] Meaning-systems are themselves a function of the human capacity for language as a symbol-bearing system. A symbol is any sign that can substitute for another, or can summarize a complex of signs or events.

Second, symbols, particularly when organized into meaning-systems, are an efficient way to store organizing patterns within the mind, and meaning-systems are effective in reducing confusion. Because symbols summarize events and meanings, they also acquire an emotional tone.

Third, humans have a relatively great capacity to *learn* behaviors, attitudes, and ideas, and relatively few preprogrammed behavioral patterns. We are, in a sense, programmed to learn. What is not programmed is *what specifically* we will learn. But we tend to learn language and store experiences in symbolic form, hence we are disposed to form meaning-systems.

Thus religion, heavily dependent on symbols, and organized as a meaning-system, gives order and meaning to experience in the same way that a political ideology, professional status, membership in a social organization, being a sports fan or a patriot can. This does not imply that religion, or any other cultural pattern is *nothing more* than a meaning-system, but only that each of these systems is a way of ordering the world. Intuitively, one may sense that being religious is somehow different from being a sports fan, a licensed social worker, or a Democrat, but it, too, works through ordinary human capacities.

Identity Formation

Religion was just defined as a system that gives order and meaning to the world. Turning to the inner person, we may look at religion as involved in important internal functions. The language that people use gives us clues. Beliefs are cherished; God, Jesus, Muhammad, and the Patriarchs (Abraham, Isaac, Jacob) are loved, feared and revered; the Bible or Qur'an is heard and listened to; forgiveness is asked and changes promised. All these images are experienced within the person in ways quite similar to the experience(s) of important people in the individual's personal history. In essence then, what we obtain psychologically from significant people in our personal odysseys parallels what we can secure from religious ideas and figures; love, values, aid in regulating our wishes and activities, a personal tradition, ethical/moral guidance, a sense of ourselves, and approval or disapproval for our thoughts and behaviors. In other words, identity.

Like the other functions and abilities discussed in this chapter, identity remains largely, if not completely, submerged below awareness. In counseling however, the identity of both parties may become a significant issue.

Questions about the counselor's identity may really be asking about acceptance, differences, fear of the counselor's control, the desire for safety, etc. Hints of the client's concerns need to be followed up in most cases, as ignoring them is frequently taken by the client to mean that such matters are "off limits."

Selected Religious Concepts

For most religious people, their religion can bear on all aspects of life. And religion has special issues and concepts that probably do not concern the nonreligious person. Just a few of these ideas, hopefully the more important ones, will be dealt with here.

Abortion

Children call upon some of our deepest, and most complex feelings. They may represent our future, and a tangible immortality. At one time children, family, and tribe were the only form of Social Security there was for nearly all humanity. Where food or other necessities are in short or uncertain supply, the birth of a child poses a danger to the rest of the family, clan, or tribe. Children also can represent aspects of ourselves that we may cherish or reject, or both.

For the most part abortion is a relatively modern issue since, as a medical procedure, it was dangerous in pre-antiseptic times. Still, certain drugs (such as ergot, naturally occurring as a fungus) and various physical intervention procedures have been tried, since early times, in order to end unwanted pregnancies.[29] Abortion was legal in the United States until about the end of the Civil War when that war's decimation, plus other factors, led to its regulation.

The current American debate over abortion is highly

charged, with secular and religious opinion taking both sides of the issue. Some advocates on each side have found support in biblical and post-biblical texts, and both sides have their share of people absolutely certain of their position. Though it was at first a one-issue movement, there are signs that some "Right-to-Lifers" have broadened their stance to include other issues, such as war, the homeless, and poverty. Some "Pro-Choicers" have similarly responded to challenges by thinking through the knotty ethical issues involved.[30] Medical technology has added to the complexity by finding potentially significant uses for fetal tissue and by making survival possible for increasingly younger fetuses.

Counselors, social workers, and therapists will inevitably have feelings about the client who presents a problem pregnancy, especially if the client asks for advice. This challenge will test the counselor's attachment to neutrality, and perhaps a word about *neutrality* is relevant here. For many nonprofessionals, neutrality often means professional indifference at best, and more likely wanton permissiveness. The issue is complex and has been treated in more detail elsewhere.[31] In brief, neutrality in the counselor does not mean indifference or permissiveness (although some counselors may embody either or both attitudes). Rather, neutrality means the counselor restrains the expression of his/her personal reactions so that the client does not receive the accustomed social signals as to what is, and is not, acceptable. Without these signals the client has to look within, finding those attitudes and feelings that are most troublesome and readily avoided.

Many people in the pregnant client's life will have strong and differing feelings about her pregnancy, and the client is also likely to feel many conflicting motives. To mention a few, pregnancy may be an occasion for shame or embarrassment for the client, or an opportunity to embarrass the client's parents, or to demonstrate her desirability, or her passage to adulthood, or to have someone to love. If the client is an adolescent, then shame or embarrassment may be the dominant emotions, but the pregnancy may also be an opportunity for the parents to retrace their early years and symbolically defer the awareness of increasing age and impending death. For the client to whom personal or parental religious affiliation is important, another set of interests is also active. If the pregnancy is the outcome of rape or incest, a much different and more terrible situation prevails.

Assuming that the counselor does not work in an agency that has a fixed position on abortion, the following is offered as one possible position through which to construe these issues:

1. Modern reproductive technology has tended to convey that the origins of life are within our understanding and control. While both of these have increased recently, reproduction and birth are *experienced* as profound events in which males can participate only vicariously, at best. When a woman decides to terminate a pregnancy, some may regard this as her wisest decision, and yet it may leave emotional residues. In counseling a client, these feelings may need considerable attention.
2. Arguments pro and con on abortion are often set on slippery grounds, not free from rationalization. Although I am personally pro-choice, the argument that a woman has a right to do whatever she wants with her body is not fully persuasive. When one's behavior impacts on others, societies tend to take an interest. Society regulates suicide, prostitution, and who can serve in a combat-status military unit. Nevertheless, that a male-dominated society has often distorted women's lives is hard to dispute.[32] Some points here are:
   a. Life probably begins before a child enters graduate school, and conception is as good a point as any other. The fertilized ovum has all of the characteristics of life, but becoming human is a slow process that only begins after birth. Thus whether a woman wishes to end or continue her pregnancy, we have competing

interests. Society may stand in for the fetus, the father or grandparents may become involved and the woman may act in her own behalf.

b. Pregnancy is a ten times greater hazard to a woman's physical health than abortion,[33] the more so if she is poor or black. Abortion is alleged to jeopardize a woman's mental health, but the evidence suggests that this is less a risk than pregnancy.[34]
c. Having more children than a family can absorb, or having them too close together can significantly affect the opportunities, growth and quality of treatment of all the children. Unwanted children are probably at more risk for abuse. Overwork, deprivation, and poverty are less likely to build character than to damage all involved.

There are many other points to be made, but these represent a few of the arguments from both sides that seem either designed to win a point or to overlook legitimate points on the other side. As these points illustrate, the client's decision frequently pivots on very difficult, painful choices, often without either a good, or a simple alternative.

Religiously based arguments are also neither simple nor immune from selections to make one's point. In Genesis, God told Adam and Eve to be fruitful and multiply, but he did not say to overpopulate. Later in the Old Testament there are injunctions that when a city is besieged, the trees should not all be destroyed; nor is the land to be continuously cultivated, but must be allowed to lie fallow one year in seven, i.e., the environment should be cared for. In Exodus 21:22, if a miscarriage is induced, as through men fighting, this is not regarded as murder unless the woman dies. Finally, the commandment against murder is often read as prohibiting killing. This is not a correct translation, as the death penalty was allowed.

Talmudic opinion was mentioned previously. The early Judeo-Christian limitation on abortion was likely part of the Jewish principle of care for the child and prohibition of either infanticide or child sacrifice. Islamic law is not different; it allows abortion to save the life of the mother, although there is a minority opinion allowing abortion up to end of the fourth month.[35]

There are few simple answers, and helping clients to come to their own understanding of their choices, consequences, and motives is probably most useful in the long run. The counselor must be as clear as possible about his or her values and recognize that to offer or assert these values to the client may leave the client with consequences the counselor does not have to shoulder.

Alcoholism

Alcoholism is a disease, with clinical findings on specialized tests, and it can be treated. But *if alcoholism is a disease, when people change their behavior, they end the "disease." What disease acts this way?*[36] These opposing views capture two main dimensions of the argument over alcoholism. If alcoholism is a disease, then people are not morally culpable; but if it is not a disease, then they are responsible for their behavior. Both positions in this argument can amass evidence to support their view. Briefly, these are:

The Disease position

1. Alcoholism has recognizable symptoms and phases. If left untreated, it will lead to physical deterioration and eventual death. In 1954, the American Medical Association unanimously voted to classify alcoholism as a disease.
2. Alcohol abuse produces definite bodily damage, including liver and brain damage, obesity, ulcers, impotence, malnutrition, and characteristic changes in the face.
3. If alcoholism *is* a disease, then treatment programs which deal with physiological, psychological, and social effects would have reasonable chances of success, and should be instituted.
4. Since most alcoholics have one or more family members

who are also alcoholic, there is a plausible argument for a genetic basis to alcoholism as a disease.

5. Chemical changes are found in the brains of alcoholics (but not in those of non-drinkers or social drinkers), in the form of a highly addictive, metabolic derivative of alcohol (tetrahydroiso-quinoline or THIQ).[37]

The Social-Behavioral position

1. Large numbers of people drink alcohol in moderation and most do not become alcoholics.[38] Those who need the sedative effects of alcohol are likely to abuse other sedative, psychoactive drugs, indicating that some psychological problem is involved.
2. Some alcoholics quit drinking, either through some sort of rehabilitation program, or on their own. The problem is behavioral, with physical effects caused by ingestion of a dangerous drug.
3. The claim of a genetic basis is derived from correlative studies and it is just as plausible to regard the prevalence of drinking behavior that runs in families as learned through modeling.
4. If alcoholism is a disease, then why is it much less frequent in cultures that embed alcohol use in a web of family and social practices and controls?[39]

I find that such arguments are more entertaining than productive. My approach is somewhat different.

1. The concept that alcoholism is a disease is useful, since it allows a rational treatment program, and blaming the substance abuser is unproductive. Since the "disease" is dependent upon individual behavior, anything that improves self-control and self-responsibility is likely to be helpful.
2. Alcoholism seems to be an end state "arrived at through a multitude of factors including genetic vulnerability, environmental stresses, social pressures, psychiatric problems, and personality characteristics."[40]
3. Since alcohol and drug abuse involve "pleasurable"[41] activi-

ties, they are harder to treat because they do not carry the pain of most other emotional problems. When a client is heavily involved in substance abuse, specialized treatment and knowledge are needed. A general counselor or therapist may need to refer the client to a specialist first, or work in tandem with a substance abuse counselor and a physician.[42]

4. Whether or not substance abuse is a disease, it causes serious and sometimes fatal physical consequences. Medical interventions may be necessary, as well as work with the family.

While the term "Demon Rum" has fallen out of favor, Islam and some Christian churches prohibit all use of alcohol, regarding any use as sinful. For clients with this background, the disease concept may be useful if it does not foster a retreat from responsibility. The Bible accepts wine (or "strong drink," perhaps beer) in moderation, while also setting limits on alcohol in a variety of texts. Even where a client's church has an official position prohibiting alcohol, pastors are nearly always cooperative and supportive when a parishioner is struggling to overcome an alcohol problem, and will usually collaborate with a substance abuse or general counselor whose approach is tactful and collaborative.

Conscientious Objector

The objection to military service is often on religious grounds, although it is occasionally made on an ethical or spiritual basis. Judaism, Christianity, and Islam all confront the issue of war and all allow for it but set certain, albeit different, limits. Peace is greatly valued by all three religions; their observance falls short of their professed ideals. Islam makes a sharp distinction between Islamic countries (The Abode of Islam) and the rest of the world (The Abode of War/Struggle)[43] but *jihad* which can mean "holy war" comes from a word meaning exertion and also means striving for moral or religious perfection. The Hebrew invasion of Canaan was sanctioned by God and the Crusades were promoted as a holy war.

Death, Grief, and Mourning

Judaism, Christianity, and Islam all see death as a major transition in life and provide rituals for mourning, comfort, and assurances for the bereaved, and explanations to their adherents. There is also a division in each religion between the standard theological position on death and how this is understood by the congregants. Initially Judaism seemed to have no concept of an afterlife, although by the start of the Common Era, the Pharisees held the idea. Theologically both mainstream Judaism and Christianity regarded what happened after death as being known only to God; but God was faithful to his people. The accretion of elaborate stories about Heaven, Purgatory, Limbo, Hell and so on were a kind of folk addition to Christianity that had little warrant in Scripture. Much of that has been tacitly dropped, but many people think that there is an immediate life after death and that those who are to be rewarded dwell with God. Some Christian denominations (Latter-Day Saints) are quite explicit about a very concrete afterlife while Christian Science appears to see disease, and perhaps death as false thinking. The Qur'an is explicit about what awaits after death.

In spite of every thing that religions provide, most people experience death as an inexplicable loss over which we have no control. Two psychological mechanisms are most readily called upon in this situation: explanations and guilt. Explanations often begin with an inquiry. Why did this evil happen to me? This is the essential question of the Book of Job, discussed in more detail in chapter 4. Guilt is also called upon for relief, strange as this may sound. We feel guilt for what we have done or failed to do, so if there was something that we did or did not do, we could have avoided this loss, hence we would not be helpless. At the price of guilt feelings we relieve our feelings of loss and helplessness. Is it worth it?

Since we cannot bring someone back to life, what can we "do" for the mourner? It is quite simple. *Be there.* It is very useful to help the person mourn, which involves remembering the good (and bad, if needed) and feeling the appropriate pain and sadness. But failure to grieve and mourn leaves one's emotions bound to a person who can no longer give anything back, and this causes consequences to the survivor. When my father died, I knew of his condition so I visited him the week before he died, about two weeks before Passover. I then returned to assist with his funeral arrangements, but didn't fully dissipate my own feelings, partly because the arrival of Passover interrupted the mourning period. Then for several years on Passover I would come down with a bad cold until a friend noticed this annual event and remarked on it. Once I made the connection, my colds ceased their annual cycle.

But is there any explanation? It may be useful to reread the answer given at the end of the Book of Job, when God answered from the whirlwind.[44] We will return to this important topic in chapter 4.

Depression

"Depression is the most widespread psychological disorder. It is the common cold of mental illness."[45] While depression, along with anxiety, is surely among the most common psychological symptoms, recognizing, understanding, and dealing with depression requires sensitivity to its many forms. The counselor needs to distinguish between specific emotional constellations, in which depressed mood is a feature, and a primary depressive problem. Thus a client who is feeling loss or stress may feel depressed, but this may not be the mainstream of their difficulties. The client who cannot get out of bed, or feels constant weariness, or cannot move or talk at an ordinary pace, or feels he is so terrible a person that some organ is rotting is one who may well be depressed—and this is not hard to see. Nor is it hard to see as depressed the client who is openly talking about suicide. But the client who is feeling tense, has trouble sleeping, has no appetite for food, experiences disruption in sexual functioning, or merely finds little enjoyment may be quite depressed too, even without a depressed mood. It is important to make a distinction between depression and sadness.

For example one 40-year-old woman was being seen because of the disintegration of her marriage, a breakup which she had initiated. After about three years of work she began to understand some of her motives, as well as to experience the consequences of her actions. She was feeling quite sad. In the midst of this, she seemed to be ill and I suggested she see a physician, who promptly diagnosed a depression and prescribed an antidepressant even though he knew she was being seen in counseling. Her sadness and depression were appropriate feelings that should not have been dampened with drugs. Another client, a rather low-key man, had been quite depressed over an arid social life. As we worked in counseling, his depression seemed a bit deeper. A colleague noted his generally "down" quality and urged him to see a physician, who diagnosed a case of pneumonia. Medication cured his pneumonia and his mood "brightened" back to its formerly low level. Nevertheless, I had partly misread his depression.

Some clients who come for counseling may have already been told they are depressed, and even that the cause is biological, and that medication can treat the problem. The recent announcement of a gene for depression has been refuted by further studies, but the issue is not dead.[46] With the remedicalization of psychiatry, this is a view gaining popularity, and is partly based on findings that some depressed people have somewhat different brain chemistries than non-depressed people. Some suspect there are political motives behind this trend too, including the pressure on psychiatry of increased competition from non-medical specialties. The implicit assumption is that the biological precedes and causes the psychological, but not the reverse. I do not know of any substantial evidence that supports this assumption consistently. That medication can alter depressive mood seems well established, but so can psychotherapy, electroconvulsive shock, and being obnoxious enough to make the client angry. For mild to moderate depressions, most reasonably benign and persistent psychological interventions help. Doing nothing may work too (although treatment is much more effective), but there are risks. The depression may become entrenched, or lack of intervention may signify to the client that no one cares, leading to increased suicidal ideas and perhaps a suicide attempt. Suicide is the major risk in depression and we will discuss this further in chapter 4.

While medication works for sixty to sixty-five percent of patients, the tricyclic antidepressants are not quick-acting, may generate annoying side effects and lead clients to see themselves as helpless, thus depleting their natural coping abilities. Lithium carbonate appears to work with manic-depressive conditions, but needs regular monitoring, since a therapeutic dose is close to the level of a toxic dose. Lithium also requires time to take effect. MAO (monoamine oxidase) is another medication that affects brain chemistry but has significant side effects, and other medications may have equivalent effectiveness. Electroconvulsive shock therapy (ECT) is quick and easy to administer, but causes brain damage, a fact that prescribers like to play down. It may also be making a comeback.[47] Also, brain damage induced by ECT makes later counseling much more difficult.

Counseling or psychotherapy is also likely to take time and may be costly, but the side effects tend to be minimal, so clients are more likely to stay and the results are as good as medication.[48] Theories of psychological causes are diverse, but it seems that many depressed people have suffered early losses of significant people. A common, though not always obvious quality is that depressed people are frequently angry, and this is particularly so in severely depressed clients.[49] Two related and currently popular cognitive psychological views suggest that clients' thoughts and expectations heavily determine their depressive outlook;[50] and that earlier experiences in which the client has felt helpless to deal with very unpleasant experiences contribute strongly to a consistently depressed mood because the person attributes negative outcomes or qualities to many events.[51] Aaron Beck's cognitive therapy pays major attention to the client's thoughts and, to the degree to which they are realistic, also considers feelings and attitudes. Counseling, which gives much attention to the client's feelings and attitudes, also considers thoughts and expectations. Skill, experience, and sensitivity appear to be the primary active factors in counseling.

Not infrequently, depressed clients will express their unhappiness in religious terms. They are sinful, are unforgivable, feel alienated from God or Jesus, or are tied to some doctrinal point. Nearly always such clients have a distorted view of their own denominations's theology. The cognitive therapy approach to the treatment of depression would point toward focusing on the negative attributions, expectations, and distortions in the client's thoughts, as in the following sample of a woman with severe headaches and a high depression score on Beck's inventory (CO = Counselor; CL = Client):

CL: My son doesn't like to go to the theatre or to the movies with me anymore.

CO: How do you know that he doesn't want to go with you?

CL: Teenagers don't actually like to do things with their parents.
CO: Have you actually asked him to go with you?
CL: No, as a matter of fact, he did ask me a few times if I wanted him to take me . . . but I didn't think he really wanted to go.
CO: How about testing it out by asking him to give you a straight answer?
CL: I guess so.
CO: The important thing is not whether or not he goes with you but whether you are deciding for him what he thinks instead of letting him tell you.[52]

Challenging a client's depressive ideas and feelings when they are expressed in religious terms is, I think, much riskier. But if the counselor utilizes a cognitive or rational-emotive approach,[53] I think that tackling religious ideas directly is less likely to be profitable than showing the client how the same feelings operate in his or her life with other people.

Devil, Satan, and Angels

The austere, imageless monotheism of ancient Israel was difficult to sustain and has been modified in various ways. *Angel* is the Greek translation of the Hebrew *malach* meaning messenger. This figure was elaborated in later Old Testament writings, acquiring specific names and characters that were developed still further in Christian and Islamic thought. The Hebrew word *satan* means adversary, hence satan was not a name at all (1 Chron. 21). When the Bible was translated, the Greek for accuser or slanderer was *diabolos*, from which we get devil. We will discuss this very important topic again under satanism in chapter 4.

These figures can have powerful meanings for some clients. In the past, Catholic parochial-school children were given the image of an invisible but continuously present guardian angel, which must have been quite mystifying, although this was largely benign and outgrown, rather like Santa Claus. The devil or Satan is depicted as a malignant figure, and can permit the client to evade responsibility for his or her behavior. For example, just recently Jim and Tammy Bakker attempted to restart their television ministry, and part of this was on a national news program. One of them explained their past and current difficulties as due to the Devil. They had been about to build the largest church in the world and would have saved too many souls. While this is a blatant example of blame-shifting, it is not uncommon. The people of the United States and Northern Ireland both report a high incidence of belief in the Devil, at sixty-six percent, followed closely by the Republic of Ireland. The other countries reported have a much lower level of belief, from thirty-three percent for Spain down to about twelve percent in Scandinavia.[54]

Discipline and Abuse

Every society has child-rearing practices that implement its values, fears, and goals and these take an unimaginable variety of forms across societies. While some societies are quite punitive with their children, others *appear* to use no discipline at all. Some are very indulgent up to a certain age, after which strict demands are imposed. Girls and boys are reared differently, to produce people fitted to their expected roles.

In many societies that are based on a fairly open, extended family, there is more diverse input into the functioning of a particular family. I think this tends to bring child-rearing practices into a narrower range, and partly corrects for the idiosyncracies of a particular set of parents. However, in a mobile, industrialized society such as the United States, the parents may so narrow the child's socialization that the parents' ideology, cultural patterns, ethnic identity, or religious beliefs may be undiluted. The impact is doubly devastating in very disturbed families, which also prevent the child from learning that others are different.

Whatever a society does to induct children into their roles and functions, these influences begin at birth with the degree to which a child is talked to, held, fed, cleaned, dressed, and treated by all members of the family. This induction process becomes a problem when it is regularly painful, with little or no corresponding comfort or reward. In this country, when the induction process painfully exceeds societal norms, we call this child abuse. Awareness of child abuse has been growing, but it is well to remember that the Society for the Prevention of Cruelty to Animals was founded before the Society for the Prevention of Cruelty to Children. Harsh treatment of children (and women) is a long-standing characteristic of Western culture.[55] It is important to know that some societies are much gentler, yet very effective in their acculturation of children.

The research literature now accumulated is clear in demonstrating that persistently abusive treatment of children has predictable effects upon their adult lives. They are much more likely to be inhibited in intimacy with others, are at increased risk to abuse their own children[56] and/or their spouse, are more vulnerable to depression, delinquency, feelings of emptiness, and are likely not to enjoy their life or successes.

But isn't it necessary to discipline children? Let us consider this very important question. *Discipline* and *disciple* both derive from the Latin for pupil, which in turn comes from the Latin verb meaning to learn. Although discipline often has meant control or punishment, it is better understood as membership in a community with similar goals and values. For example, in the university, the various areas of study (physics, economics, psychology, etc.) are called disciplines. It was wisely observed that "love is the final basis of all authority,"[57] and it is this perspective that informs what follows. Briefly, when a parent acts in ways that contribute to a child's growth, conveys a sense of affection, concern, and respect for the child, and provides, to the extent possible, an appropriately structured environment, I consider this to be love. Love can entail setting appropriate goals and limits, as well as supporting possibilities, and sometimes demanding achievements.

Many of the severe punishments given to children come from parental frustration, and raising children is sometimes frustrating. Parents who have themselves been poorly parented, single parents, or parents weighed down by illness, or economic or social deprivation are also at risk for abusive behavior. To set some balance here, I want to note that children are not fragile glass sculptures and a single unnecessarily harsh interaction is rarely devastating.

But doesn't the Bible teach "spare the rod and spoil the child"[58] and "honor your father and mother?" Injunctions toward punishment are repeated in numerous places (Proverbs 13:24, 19:18, 22:15, 23:13–14, 29:15 and Ecclesiasticus 30:1–13). Such frequent repetition suggests that harsh punishment was *not* the norm, but that kindliness and indulgence was more the practice in biblical times. But in the New Testament, St. Paul, while urging children to obey parents, also counseled parents not to nag, anger or arouse resentment in their children (Ephesians 6:1–4, Colossians 3:20–21, I Thessalonians 2:11–12).

What about honoring one's parents? While we will deal with biblical translations in the last chapter, it is important to know that people in biblical times had a quite different understanding of their world and that translating a language two to four thousand years old is a difficult and daunting task. What did they mean by "honor your parents?" Honor seems to have derived from a word meaning weighty or glorify. Thus honoring one's parents seems to have meant to treat parents with respect (or courtesy), or act in a way to bring credit (glory) to them. Since there were words for love and obedience, and these were not used in the Ten Commandments, it may be that children were asked to do only what was possible.

Grace, Healing, and Salvation

All three words trace back through Old English, German or Latin to the Proto-Indo-European language.[59] Healing and salvation have similar meanings (whole, hale, or uninjured), and it seems to have been physical healing as well as spiritual aid that was sought from Jesus. Grace may have at first meant oral praise, but evolved to mean favor or pleasing. Now grace has come to connote divine aid leading to salvation which, in the Christian view, rescues the person from the evil of the world, and perhaps from the "fallen" state of humanity, consistent with the concept of original sin. Different Christian denominations place different emphases on these terms, but salvation ("Have you been saved?") seems a currently favored test of another person's faith-position for conservatives, evangelicals, or fundamentalists.

Holy Spirit

The Holy Spirit or Holy Ghost is the third aspect of the Trinity and was a more gradual development in Christian theology. God operates through the Holy Spirit in most Christian thought, while Jews and Muslims tend to see God's effect on the world more directly, or through the medium of angels (messengers). I suspect that the modern attachment to the concept of the Holy Spirit expresses an experience of God's greater distance. For many members of churches in the conservative spectrum,[60] the experience of grace or salvation is conveyed through immersion or baptism in the Holy Spirit. This common expression does not, in itself, indicate particular problems.

Reports of direct experiences with God are uncommon, and would suggest a potential for more serious personal disturbance.

Homosexuality

Sexual behavior in many animal species is largely or fully organized by the genetic program of the animal, although experience can modify that program even below the primate level.[61] In humans, the matter is much more complex, with both experience and constitutional factors interacting in intricate, and as yet incompletely understood ways. Many people regard heterosexuality as "normal" and homosexuality as an error, sin, abnormality, or choice.[62] This last view is advanced by gay groups that characterize homosexual, bisexual, or heterosexual behavior as a preference or lifestyle. In my experience, sexual orientation is neither a choice nor a preference but has all the characteristics of a compulsion. People can exert some choice as to whether or not to engage in sexual behavior under certain circumstances, but feelings resist conscious control.

Powerful political influences are active regarding sexual attitudes and behavior. They bear upon whether to diagnose homosexuality as a disorder or not,[63] how much money to appropriate to the treatment and prevention of AIDS,[64] confidentiality in disclosing the diagnosis of AIDS or its precursors, whether gay and lesbian[65] groups may have specially-designated masses or other church activities, and so on. For most clients, sexuality will sooner or later become an issue in counseling—to be avoided, faced, understood, and transformed. Some perspective on sexuality helps the counselor work with this, and what I find most useful is given here and in the next section.

A sexual orientation is very difficult (at best) to modify, and gay or lesbian clients who come for counseling are most likely to do so for the same reasons as do straight clients; depression, relationship problems, self-esteem difficulties, and such. For the counselor to try to change a sexual orientation when the client does not present that as a problem is unethical. Probably futile too. What is more likely is that clients present conflicts between sexual thoughts, wishes, or behavior and their religious orientation. However, one quite troubled man I was working with began to engage in homosexual activity as his marriage was unraveling. Although he was reluctant, I persuaded him to describe the details of this. While he engaged in anal intercourse, he did so lying on his back, with his partner on top in a way that was both strenuous and painful. I said to him that I thought he wanted to have his father's love (a problem we had discussed before) but did not know any other way to be close to a man. He quickly discontinued this activity.

When the Bible's statements on homosexuality are considered, they *seem* very clear—for men.[66] Female homosexuality is never mentioned in the Old Testament, while references in the New Testament are vague and rare. This is not because women were unimportant, as has been suggested, because other sexual activities involving women are regulated.[67] Just what the writers of the Bible had in mind is often difficult to recover because the modern reader must try to recover the specific social context.[68] In the Old Testament it seems likely that ritual sexuality in pagan religions was the specific target of these prohibitions, but the attitude of a partly agricultural society toward "wasting seed" was also a factor.

In New Testament times, Greco-Roman attitudes and practices are the dominant theme, yet the Gospels, Acts and the Book of Revelation seem unconcerned with homosexuality. Careful reading of I Corinthians indicates that there are three lists of vices, a literary device St. Paul employed. Only the third list (I Corinthians 6:9–10) refers to homosexuality, and this is not given special attention. Rather, it appears to heighten the impact of St. Paul's letter.[69] In Romans 1:18–32, where St. Paul makes a clearer and more systematic statement on homosexuality, a careful study of the language, the customary practices of his time, and the criticisms of homosexuality by pagan writers demonstrates that the nearly universal model of homosexuality was pederasty ("love of boys"). It seems most likely that St. Paul was attacking the exploitative, dehumanizing, forced pederasty also condemned by many pagan writers. St. Paul might have also condemned the modern model of adult, caring mutual homosexuality, but there is no way to know.[70] Finally, it is important to be aware that *the Bible does not forbid homosexuality, only homosexual acts.*

Pleasure and Sex

Most people view sexuality as an impulse that drives the person, or an impulse the person must resist or control. Experientially, sex can have that quality. Also, there are complex bodily structures and mechanisms, secretions and cycles, all of them important to sexual functioning. Yet nearly all of sexual functioning is brain-based,[71] and much is determined by the mind and the social situation. Thus sexual intercourse in public is very rare. The degree to which a person is attractive depends on their category (degree of relation, age, gender), and lack of sexual satisfaction is not fatal. True drives *require* satisfaction, such as for air, water, and food. If the person is deprived beyond the organism's capacity to sustain itself, such frustration is fatal. Not so for sexuality, although sexual deprivation may be quite unpleasant. Adult humans can remain sexually competent even if the ovaries or testicles are removed, since sexual intercourse is not activated by female fertility. Human sexual response is powerfully influenced by psychological factors. Both men and women may be capable of sexual activity without orgasm, and both may be unable to perform entirely because of psychological factors. In brief then, sex involves human *relationships.* Even masturbation usually involves fantasies.

Sexuality, while not synonymous with intimacy, is configured by the nature of the person's relationships with others, past experiences and their meanings, the person's view of the self, and certain common psychological mechanisms. For example, after a rape a woman may find sex frightening, and experience flashbacks, emotional withdrawal, grief, self-blame, and other understandable reactions. What about the woman who becomes sexually provocative after rape? This is actually her attack on her fears in which she symbolically reverses her prior helplessness, saying, "See? I caused the rape, I have control, I can choose this." Hence sex may be a vehicle to confirm one's worth, worthlessness, attractiveness, repulsiveness, or other meanings.

Extramarital sexual activity has a similarly diverse range of meanings. One client had almost no sexual relations with his wife for nearly a decade because of her reluctance. In spite of severe sexual frustration he did not engage in affairs; while another client had a brief affair after more than fifteen years of a very satisfying sexual relationship with his wife. In the first instance, counseling partly dealt with what led this man to tolerate his situation for so long, while in the second, I first explored what was going on when the affair started. Here we found that his wife was undertaking training that would have made her more independent, changing their relative status. He was threatened and the affair seemed to restore a sense of worth. I have never seen a client whose motive for an extramarital affair was primarily understandable as due to sexual frustration, although many clients experience that as the apparent motive.

What of the client who has had an affair, or affairs, and feels guilt, particularly guilt based on having transgressed biblical commandments? I find it helpful to try to examine with the client what the affair was about; that is, what symbolic meaning did it have? One client had some affairs after his wife's behavior hurt his self-esteem, as well as reminding him of his rather prudish mother. His affairs were a revenge against his mother, personified by his wife. Judaism, Islam, and Christianity all offer ample means to expiate guilt. Confession is one attractive alternative, but this contains the possibility for the expression of hidden hostility on the part of the confessing person. Such a disclosure needs careful consideration.

Sexual attraction or repulsion is experienced as a fact, arising from the charms of the other person. It is never this simple. "Beauty is in the eye of the beholder" is roughly true, but incomplete. Attraction is often based on past experiences, which create a template that strongly contributes to what people find attractive or not attractive. One client described her ex-husband's negative relationship with his domineering, hostile mother. Before and during their marriage, the husband had been arrested for exposing himself and had had several extramarital affairs. She was a slender, small-breasted woman, and was surprised when I surmised that her former mother-in-law was quite buxom.[72] Understandably, her husband wished to avoid a woman who would remind him of his mother.

Strong emotional or physical attraction feels imperative to a client and may be called chemistry, needing no further explanation. Such emotional dictates can withstand the scrutiny of counseling if the attraction is substantially founded in the person's current life. Where the person's attractions are mainly rooted in old emotional patterns that are not congruent with current needs and situations, exploring the bases of sudden fascinations can be useful, even if disenchanting to the client.

Love, Marriage, Annulment, and Divorce

Human love is, perhaps, one of the great enigmas of mortal existence but its reality, twists and turns, beauties, and follies are recorded in clear-eyed fashion in the Old Testament. The ancient Hebrews had no qualms about the value and pleasure of sexual love between adults but required a standard of behavior that bounded such love within the family, approving it between husband and wife and forbidding it with children, relatives, as a religious act, or between men. Curiously, while men are regularly shown in love with their wives, only one woman (Saul's daughter Michal, who married David) is shown directly to have loved her husband, and her end was tragic.

In Jewish life, marriage is a contractual relationship that provides satisfaction, mutual care, help and support, rearing of children, and a structure within which the religious life of the family can flourish. The numbers of wives Old Testament patriarchs and kings were allowed have long since been narrowed to one. The Talmud regarded sexual satisfaction as a joint right of both husband and wife. Divorce, once easily obtained by a man's issuance of a written divorce, now requires action by a rabbinic court. Since Jewish marriages are not made in heaven, it is not hard to secure a Jewish divorce (*get*), but divorce is regarded as a major failure and the divorced partners may not remarry each other. Even with the relative ease of Jewish divorce, it is only in recent times that Jewish divorce rates have begun to approach the national average. Jewish parents are more likely to worry about intermarriage than divorce. If a Jewish couple secures a civil divorce, but fails to get a religious divorce, any children born of a subsequent union are under the most severe ban Jewish law imposes. A child born of an incestuous or adulterous relationship is a *mamzer*, often mistranslated as bastard. Such a child can only marry others of the same status, placing a devastating burden on the child.

The early church, as it formulated Christian views of marriage, chose between the two conflicting statements of Jesus in the Gospels (Matthew 19, vs. Mark 10 and Luke 16), and decided that divorce was not permissible.[73]

Modern readers of these ancient Jewish and Christian texts may find them offensive, but they represented progressive attempts in both traditions to improve the rights and position of women from possessions to people, albeit not on a par with men. Both Judaism and Christianity regarded procreation as a primary purpose of marriage but took different approaches to the preservation of the marital unit. The Catholic position recognizes annulment which is sometimes misunderstood as saying the marriage did not exist and hence the children are illegitimate. Rather, annulment means that the necessary conditions of marriage have not been met; lack of consummation, lack of understanding, or inability to live out the ideals of marriage.

Islamic law views marriage as "a legal commitment sanctioned by God and acknowledged by society."[74] Although clergy is not required under Islamic law, marriage is both a religious and a civil act that leads, ideally, to children, family, companionship and sexual satisfaction. Homosexuality and celibacy are rejected. Choice of a spouse is a matter that involves the entire family, and the partners, particularly the women, may have little or much to say, depending on the culture—although in theory both should consent. Similarly, women have many rights and equal status under Islamic law, but the implementation of this varies from one society to another. In the United States, it seems likely that the assimilative process will work even on families from other countries; American converts to Islam are likely to develop practices that are an amalgam of typical American customs, informed and modified by Islamic law. Thus, while a Muslim man can theoretically have up to four wives,[75] civil United States law would be determining. One to a customer.

Divorce in Islam is theoretically easy, although strongly discouraged, and in this regard rather like Jewish law. Under Jewish law a woman cannot divorce her husband, although she can sometimes compel him to divorce her.

In Islam, a woman's right to divorce can be written into the marriage contract, and even if not, a divorce can be compelled under specific circumstances.

In many ancient cultures religious law *was* civil law, but as societies incorporated disparate religions, an increasing distinction grew up. In the United States, the distinction is almost complete, and while marriage and divorce (or annulment) may involve a religious legal procedure, action in the civil area does not satisfy the requirements in the religious. For this reason, many people have to satisfy both state and religious requirements.

Women and Men

Gender is so pervasive in the natural world that one needs to go nearly to one-celled animals to find this feature suspended. Among some species the female is dominant (many insects, certain reptiles, and fish), but within the mammalian kingdom, where male and female are pair-bonded beyond the mating cycle,[76] the predominant pattern seems to be male domination below the primate level. With humans there is more variability; in nomadic and hunter-gatherer societies, males and females have more similar functions and tend to be largely equal in status. In agricultural societies, males tend to be predominant. This is all quite ironic since the basic human genetic pattern is female; males are a variant and because they do not have the second X chromosome, they are more vulnerable to disease, die younger, and seem to have higher rates of sex-linked genetic disorders. In a word, men are the weaker sex, except for average differences in muscle and bone bulk. To say that men are dominant because this is the natural order or divinely ordained is to beg the question.

The role and status of women in ancient times varied, but it appears that in ancient Greece, Spartan women had much independence, while in Athens they were secluded and protected under male guardianship all their lives.[77] During Hellenistic and later times, women gradually assumed more control of their lives. In Athens and Rome, marriage was decided for a woman by her father, who also could unilaterally compel her to divorce. Although either a man or a woman could divorce without social disapproval, it was much easier for men than for women to initiate. It was several centuries before a woman had much say about a marriage, and that was mainly outside of Athens. Roman law gave the father power of life and death over the entire family; women were thus subject to unregulated male control, although this too waned through the centuries.

This is the backdrop to Jewish, Christian, and Islamic views and regulation of women. Women are portrayed, characterized and regulated in the Bible and Qur'an, but the writing was by men. Perhaps if women had had their say, then one quarter of the Talmud[78] would not have been devoted to the topic of *Nashim* (Women). Yet the unbridled control of women in Athens or Rome contrasts with the complex portrait given in these Scriptures. Two views of women are given in the beginning of Genesis; In Chapter 1 God created male and female without suggestion of different status but in the second chapter we have the famous story of woman being created from Adam's rib. I think this represents an ancient awareness of both the usual difference between men and women, and also recognition of the less common event of woman being a force equal to man. A woman's consent to marriage is deduced from Genesis 24:55–58[79] and her capacity for independent business activity is clearly described in Proverbs 31:10–31. The corrosive hatred of women in some classical Greek and Roman writers far exceeds any negative attitudes in Scripture. Thus the Old Testament took a more humane and complex view of women—one that seemed relatively insulated from Greek and Roman law and practice.

The New Testament, set within the Greco-Roman world, was exposed to then-current standards. Jesus associated with both men and women with remarkable openness and acceptance. St. Paul was quite radical in some statements on equality of men and women; others, such as in Ephesians, have been taken to mean that women were to be subservient to men. St. Paul's meaning is seen to be more complex once these passages are compared in several translations, especially with explanatory comments. The most radical position on equality of women and men before God (Allah) is found in the Qur'an,[80] although many countries that are predominantly Muslim tend to follow local customs rather than Qur'anic law and the Hadith.[81] There is severe feminist Muslim critique of actual practices, a selection of which is found in *Islam from Within*.[82]

With the exception of Mary Baker Eddy (Christian Science) and Ellen White (Seventh-Day Adventist) in this country, the involvement of most women in religious life has been subordinate to men.[83] Many Protestant denominations ordain women as ministers; the struggle is often over whether a woman can be a bishop. The Reform and Conservative movements in Judaism accept women as rabbis; Orthodox Judaism is not expected to change any time soon.[84] In the Roman Catholic church women have long served in lay orders as teaching and nursing nuns, and currently serve as lectors and administrators too. The American Catholic hierarchy has firmly but respectfully disagreed with the Vatican on an expanded role for women.[85] The Vatican is not expected to change any time soon.

Feminist critiques of modern society have concentrated primarily on the possibilities women have been excluded from. It is worth noting that men's roles inhibit their release of anguished feelings through crying or being comforted, impose the obligation to earn a living (often through better paying, but high-stress work), impair their capacity to access the full range of human feelings (often valuable for their informational and motivational qualities), and impede a reasonable sense of self-worth based on satisfaction with realistic but not superlative accomplishment. In brief then, competitive-dominating, punitive-withholding relationships between men and women end up depriving both. The traditional female-male socialization patterns make stress on both a likely adult problem. The role training of many men leaves them feeling vulnerable and threatened by pressure for changes from their partners without any compensatory advantages. Counseling in such situations needs to be sensitive to the needs and fears of both partners, and aware that there are mutual advantages to adjustments in role patterns.

I have seen a couple of instances where "enlightened" parents decided to avoid confining male-female stereotypes in raising their own children. Instead of encouraging diversity in play, toy choice, emotional patterning, and so on, they disrupted anything on the child's part that smacked of role-specific behavior. The child experienced a confused self-image, with little sense of what was appropriate or effective social behavior. Relationships with peers were poor, school achievement was disorganized, and anxiety pervaded the child's experience. There is a difference then, between narrow stereotypes and a coherent sense of self which includes gender identity.

Does the Bible or Qur'an set males in positions of power? A simple yes or no is not possible because the Bible itself was written over a span of more than a thousand years, contains several distinct parts and several types of texts, was written in three languages and lives in numerous cultures. While the scriptural views of women were complex, men wielded power most of the time, although powerful women are recognized, especially in the narrative portions of the Old Testament. The Qur'an was only written in one language over a short period of time, but it, too, lives in numerous cultures.

The story of Eve is commonly employed to justify the oppression of women but this is based on what I think is a biased reading of the story. In brief, both Adam and Eve eat the forbidden fruit, but only the serpent and Adam are cursed. Eve and Adam are also punished; for Eve the pain of giving birth is *increased*, and for Adam the difficulty of agricultural labor is *increased*[86] but Eve's punishment is probably lighter than Adam's. This view contradicts the usual reading of this part of the Bible, but is more consistent with an objective reading of this text. I think that Eve's punishment was lighter because she accepted some responsibility, while Adam blamed Eve.

Emotional Problems, Prayer, and Treatment

The English word comes from the Latin *precari* meaning to ask earnestly, and so the common meaning of prayer is to ask God. Some people object to indulging in a game of "gimme," even with God, and certainly some worshippers seem to abuse or debase the process of prayer. But the origin of prayer in the Bible is more interesting. In Hebrew, prayer is *tefillah* which is from the infinitive *pallel* meaning to pray, judge, or examine. In this conjugation, prayer may be taken to mean to review one's self, or self-examination.

"If you pray hard enough your problems will be relieved" or words to that effect are not uncommon among certain religious people. Counselors may dismiss such statements, yet there are similarities between prayer and counseling beyond those described above. Both intend to make changes within the person's life through a verbal dialogue between two people (client and counselor, or worshipper and God or minister). In prayer, the congregant typically asks for help or guidance, but prayer can include confession, contrition, adoration, or self-examination. In counseling, the client also asks for help or advice, and may disclose painful, hidden experiences (confession), express regret or remorse (contrition), or may disclose intense positive feelings about the counselor or some other person (adoration). All this can promote self-examination.

What, then, are the differences? Prayer deals with moral or spiritual problems while counseling deals with problems in living. There is overlap, since moral or spiritual problems often are problems in living. It seems that the primary difference is the focus. In prayer the worshipper attempts to communicate with God or someone who can help apply God's messages to humanity within the cultural system of the individual. In counseling, clients are helped to discern their own meanings and purposes in order to become more whole and less conflicted. Counseling is commonly criticized as being self-centered, while prayer is God-centered. Temporarily true; the goal of being more whole and less conflicted is to be free of too much *or* too little concern with the self, and to have an increased capacity for relationships with others.

While counseling does not directly address moral or ethical concerns unless the client raises them, the common charge that counseling or psychotherapy is value-free is false. The client is encouraged to tell the *truth.*[87] The kinds of relationships that clients are able to have after successful counseling are essentially those prescribed by most moral and ethical systems. The difference, then, is less the outcome than the approach. For the person with truly spiritual concerns, counseling may be less effective than spiritual direction, while for the person with emotional problems, prayer may be less effective than counseling. The clash between the two seems to arise mainly from two competing world-views.

Miracles

This word is another example of how modern and ancient ideas differ. Miracle comes from the Latin *miraculum* while the Bible uses words that mean sign, wonder, or act of power. The modern meaning of miracle suggests a supernatural change in the natural world, while the biblical descriptions usually narrate natural events. The crossing of the Reed Sea (not the Red Sea, as most people think) described how a strong wind (and possibly tide) blowing across a shallow body of water produced a temporary drop in the water level. Boaters on Lake Erie are familiar with this event. *Manna* is the sticky exudate of an insect native to the area, while the "burning bush" is a shrub whose volatile sap has a low ignition temperature. The sap vaporizes and can burn without being hot enough to destroy the plant. Thus these ancient peoples were less concerned with what an event *was* than what it was *for*.[88] These signs could legitimize a person's claim to be a messenger from God, or be a sign of the presence of God, but they were typically directed to a community even when experienced by an individual.

Today miracles are regarded as supernatural events and they are often sought as a special sign of God's love and closeness. Some ministers of my acquaintance will occasionally recount devout and enthusiastic parishioners who pray for a parking space and take finding one as a sign of God's care. While they are ruefully amused, it seems that clients who need this "sign" are bereft indeed. In counseling, attempting to argue with, or even ridicule such needs is heartless. It is more useful to recognize the need expressed and look for relevant antecedents, such as neglectful or abusive parents.

Parents and Children

Human conflict is a recurrent biblical theme; between tribal groups, men and women, kings and people, prophets and leaders, brothers and sisters, husbands and wives, and parents and children. Conflict is narrated in the various stories, counseled in the Wisdom literature (Proverbs, Ecclesiastes, Ecclesiasticus), and regulated in the law of the Old Testament and the advice of St. Paul in the New Testament. Where there is love in a relationship, conflict is nearly certain, and feelings will be complex. The closer the relationship the more intense and knotty will be the feelings, and the problems in dealing with them. As with any other part of the Bible, to simply apply the portion one prefers, in the translation one is familiar with, to the problem at hand is to make a misuse likely. It is important to try to understand the intent of the writer and the context of his time and to realize that we refract the original text through the spectacles of tradition.

A few points to be noted about commonly used biblical injunctions on the relations between parents and children. "Honor your father and your mother, that you may live long in the land which the Lord your God is giving you"[89] is a most familiar commandment, but what might it mean? As was mentioned before, "honor" is a word that may be translated as "weighty" or "glorify," but does not mean love or obedience. To go a step beyond our previous discussion, this commandment contains a reason—to "live long in the land." While modern readers may find the presence of reasons unremarkable, they are rarely given in the Old Testament. Hence the presence of a reason implies this commandment is specially distinctive and, simply, this seems to mean that the integrity of the family promotes the survival of the society.

Some angry parents rely on a selection of biblical writings to justify excessively harsh treatment of their children. Where the parent is not too entrenched in this attitude, gentle pointing out of countervailing verses may help. If parents express the view that they are commanded to follow these rules, then the motives involved are externalized, and arguing with other biblical texts is fruitless and may alienate the client. Possible ways to step around this sort of position are discussed in chapter 5. The prior section on discipline and abuse is relevant here, too.

Poverty and Wealth

There are a number of conditions in life, such as poverty or wealth, illness or health, and calamity or good fortune, that seem to happen without any explanation. In the musical *Fiddler on the Roof* Tevye sings the famous song, "If I Were a Rich Man," in which he both entreats and challenges God on his poverty. Yet Tevye declares that his position is part of God's "vast, eternal plan," while lamenting his lot. Many people would agree, and it is only within the last two centuries that human ability to substantially modify the environment has bloomed. Before the invention of the steamboat, the railroad, the telegraph, and the telephone—all within the nineteenth century, communication and transportation were no faster than in Roman times, and often slower. It is only in the last century or so that there has been any reason to believe that humans could control their environment except in very limited ways, and that not all was within God's control.

Life and death, so much more subject to human intervention than in the past, is still not fully within human control and may never be. Our environment has been affected in non-benign ways, as smog-filled cities and a deteriorating ozone layer attest. Our evolving grasp of human behavior (including thoughts and feelings), and the newer methodologies (counseling, psychotherapy, behavior therapy, behavioral medicine) to temper such behavior have begun to remake our understanding of ourselves in ways we cannot foresee. Once a nearly fixed matter, one's station in life is now understood to be comprised of many components including intelligence, opportunity, and motivation, some of which are alterable, albeit with difficulty. Counselors thus regard the capacity to change as a basic principle and, confronted with a client whose view is that all is as God wills it, are likely to regard such a stance as pathological. Here, as elsewhere, it is more useful to consider this the client's expression of his or her life experience.

For example, one client I had seen for marital problems had made some temporary progress in her relationship with her husband, which led to a mutual sexual encounter. Describing this event in negative terms, she mentioned "the plan." I inquired and she connected this to her early religious training on the role of women as sexual service-providers. Perhaps as much as anything, she resented the feeling that she had done what she was supposed to and had lost control of the situation. Arguing with a client over whether he or she has unnecessarily surrendered control is likely to be fruitless. Exploring the meanings to the client is more likely to lead to movement and growth.

Sin

Sin is defined as deliberately violating God's law, yet this was not the original meaning. Sins could be unknown[90] and yet require repentance and sacrifice. *Het*,[91] as mentioned earlier, is the common word for sin in Hebrew and, most simply, means an error. Deliberate sin in either the Old or New Testament is designated by other words that are much less frequently used. Unintentional sin was recognized as common and although sacrifice was specified, this was not construed as a punishment, but as recompense, rather like civil damages.[92]

An intense concern about sin in a client may reflect one or more types of difficulties. Where the client has actually significantly injured another person, some sort of restitution or apology may be appropriate. In instances where an extramarital affair has occurred, some clients feel impelled to confess as part of the restitution process. Where the spouse is unaware of the affair, such action may cause much further difficulty. Restitution can occur without the other person being aware, whereas direct disclosure may contain unresolved hostility on the part of the client. If restitution or apology does not satisfy the client, then something else is likely at work and needs investigation.

A client's intense sense of sinfulness may indicate strong anger directed toward someone in the client's life, but with the anger redirected toward the client to avoid self-awareness. Another fairly frequent problem is expressed as a striving for perfection. Clients often feel burdened by this internal goad toward perfection and I find reassurance or support to be of little help. It may even be counter-productive since you will sound like everyone else. I may say, "Perfection is the antidote for worthlessness," as a way to open an inquiry into such painful feelings. An alternative I also find useful is to say, "You seem to have a defect in your conscience." Since most such people are actually fairly scrupulous about their behavior, this provocative remark gets their attention. I point out that "A conscience should do three things; warn you against doing wrong, make you feel badly if you do wrong, and reward you when you do well. Your conscience does fine on the first two but fails on the third."

Some clients may rely on two nearly parallel statements in Matthew (5:48) and Luke (6:36). In Matthew, Jesus enjoins people to "be perfect just as your heavenly Father is perfect" (Jerusalem Bible), or "there must be no limit to your goodness . . .(New English Bible), or "Be true." . . (Anchor Bible). However Lamsa[93] renders "be perfect" as "All inclusive. To know all lines of a trade." suggesting that Matthew and Luke may have used an Aramaic word that could mean "whole" and "generous."[94]

Other clients have developed a detailed and specific list of sins of all sorts. While Jewish practice tends to focus on specific behavioral prescriptions and prohibitions, detailed lists of sins are really inconsistent with either Jesus or St. Paul. They were much more concerned with the internal attitudes and feelings than with behavioral trivia, with alienation from God rather than ritual devoid of meaning. Nevertheless, such clients may be communicating their sense of alienation from God and from important people in their lives. Their sense of badness can express their explanation of others' mistreatment, neglect, and hostility. I find that trying to open such feelings up is initially painful, but if the counselor does so in a manner that expresses interest in the client's feelings without endorsing the accuracy of the feelings, then a healing process can be initiated.

4

Special Challenges of Religious Expression

What is a Cult

Next to terrorism, the Ayatollah Khomeini and AIDS, many people place cults in society's current Pantheon of Frights. How realistic are these fears? Do we need to worry that our children will be stolen by "trolls?" Who are these Pied Pipers? Can deprogrammers save our children? To answer these questions, first let us summarize our discussion of cults in chapter 1. One definition refers to a special interest group in the Roman Catholic church. In the sociology of religion, a *church* refers to a religious grouping that is connected with the outside world, a *sect* is a group that has split off from a church and withdrawn from its social environment, while a *cult* is an innovative religious group.

In common use however, the term cult is loaded with such negative meanings that *new religious movement*[1] (NRM) will be used for the most part, to try to encourage a more objective look at the nature of these new religions, who they attract, how well they retain members, and what concerned parents or others may want to do about a person they care for who has joined an NRM. Judaism, Christianity, and Islam were all once NRMs, but after more or less turbulent beginnings, settled down into broad movements that embraced diverse types of people.

Some Current New Religious Movements

NRMs are not new to the United States, nor is their persecution. Current NRMs are very diverse, and are frequently in conflict with the interests of other elements in society. Two experienced sociologists, Bromley and Shupe reviewed the history of five religions (Mennonite, Shaker, Mormon, Jehovah's Witnesses, Roman Catholic) that were vilified and persecuted. They noted five characteristics attributed to these denominations that are applied today to current NRMs:

1. deception and coercion used to recruit and hold members,
2. illegitimacy of beliefs,
3. sexual perversion,
4. political subversion, and
5. financial exploitation.[2]

If the names of groups being attacked are removed, it is frequently impossible to tell which group is under attack just from the content of the criticism.

The Children of God

The Children of God (COG) began quietly enough as Teens for Christ (a coffeehouse ministry) in 1968 under the leadership of David Berg, himself an ordained minister of the fundamentalist Christian and Missionary Alliance. Berg developed a semi-nomadic program, traveling from city to city, selling literature and appealing mainly to disaffected and alienated teenagers and adults in their twenties. Membership in the mid-seventies was estimated at about 4,000–5,000 members worldwide, with less than 1,000 in the United States. The theology of this church is not well organized but sees the present as the end-time (millennial and eschatological), based on a prophesied series of events, some of which have already been outstripped by actual events.

The Unification Church of America

The Unification Church of America (UCA) is the American branch of the Holy Spirit Association for the Unification of World Christianity, founded by the Reverend Sun Myung Moon in 1954. Like the COG, the UCA claims to be the true Christianity, but it is much more structured and theologically coherent than the COG. While Jesus's salvific death is acknowledged, the Trinity is rejected and the UCA's theology is focused on the failure of Adam and Eve to develop the perfect spiritual family after Eve's seduction by Lucifer. The UCA is also millennial and Moon expects a second coming of a messiah, perhaps Moon himself. The refractory nature of human history has also necessitated the revision of the Reverend Moon's timetable of events a couple of times.

Moon moved to the United States in 1971 to concentrate his efforts here, and this activated intense interest. Relatively large numbers of young people were "converted," but their involvement tended to burn out quickly and the UCA's estimate of 5,000–7,000 members in the mid-seventies may since have shown some growth. Nevertheless, dropouts have continued to occur. In spite of a conviction for income tax evasion, Moon and the UCA have sought influence in a variety of ways by aligning with conservative causes.[3] The UCA has had a propensity for shooting itself in the foot, and its current political efforts seem no exception.

Hare Krishna

The International Society for Krishna Consciousness (ISKCON or Hare Krishnas) originated from a Hindu sect that began in fifteenth century India. The movement was brought to this country in 1965 by a retired Indian businessman, A. C. Bhaktivedanta Swami Prabhupada, who died in 1977. The Hare Krishnas are monotheistic, as is Hindu theology, even though God is represented in three aspects (Brahmin or creator, Siva or destroyer, and Vishnu or preserver). Krishna is an aspect of Vishnu. The group's theology differs from orthodox Hindu thought in emphasizing the individuality of Krishna. Membership is estimated to be 3,000 to 4,000.

The Divine Light Mission

The Divine Light Mission (DLM) was brought to the United States in 1971 by Guru Maharaj Ji, descendant of a line of gurus (masters). Early on he was regarded as having special talents, and at age 8 was appointed titular head of the DLM. He arrived in this country as a young adolescent, generating intense interest. Although some 50,000 people were exposed to Maharaj Ji's teachings of the "Knowledge," membership in the mid-seventies was estimated to be under 1,500. Theologically, the DLM holds there is One Reality in which all take part. All the major religions are "true" since they all relate to "Knowledge."

The Church of Scientology

The Church of Scientology was started by science fiction writer L. Ron Hubbard and resembled a popularization of basic psychoanalytic concepts attached to a computer-like model of the mind. Purporting to bring about a "clear" through a few hours of "auditing," it was received with intense interest and enthusiasm in 1950. This early promise was not fulfilled, but in the early fifties Hubbard added spiritual dimensions (including reincarnation and life on other worlds), to his ideas, which coalesced in the Church of Scientology. Through a variety of steps, Hubbard acted to centralize and maintain control of his church and by the 1960s his organization was well-structured. Bromley and Shupe reported membership figures as being only in several tens of thousands, but this figure seems low.

The People's Temple

The People's Temple of Jim Jones began in a quite ordinary fashion in the early fifties as a ministry to poor and deprived people, offering soup kitchens, day care, and drug counseling. Jones was eventually ordained as a minister of the Disciples of Christ in 1964. He emphasized racial equality, which earned some enmity and harassment from nonmembers. He moved several times, eventually gathering a large following as he managed his several church locations. Feeling persecuted, and working mainly with casualties of the economic system, Jones was attracted to socialism, which he incorporated into his thinking. His theology began as a standard fundamentalism but evolved into an idiosyncratic theology, including the idea of suicide as a revolutionary act. He moved most of his members (some 900) to Jonestown in Guyana where his authoritarian control tightened. This culminated in the dramatic and tragic mass suicide through drinking poisoned Kool-Aid.

Issues About New Religious Movements

Why Do They Join?

From the perspective of the (often young) convert, there is immediate acceptance, warmth, and purpose. Competitiveness is rejected, basic needs (food and shelter) are taken care of, and the new convert's contribution can be felt immediately. Idealism is strong, giving the feeling that one is involved in a new, developing program, untainted by the readily observed, sordid, self-serving motives of society.

One may wonder if this is enough of an explanation, since most late adolescents and young adults do *not* join NRMs. If we consider what emotional investments do for people, the matter may be clearer. As we discussed in chapter 3 in defining religion, it can provide meaning and order to the person's life, and a sense of connection with others. When there is an intense, passionate attachment to other people, these attachments strengthen the person's personality, supplement a sense of self-worth and ability to deal with the inevitable frustrations of living, and fortify control over impulses that would violate the person's values.[4] For people who need this attachment to stabilize a precarious sense of self, attempts to interfere with their attachments are experienced as a severe threat to their personal integrity and emotional coherence. Such threats are strongly resisted.

Brainwashing, Deceptive Recruiting, Violence, and Fund Raising

A common accusation against the new religions is that they engage in "brainwashing," thought reform, deception, and other unethical techniques to recruit and capture members. The literature on brainwashing shows that it requires considerable control of the person, is highly expensive and ineffective.[5] Deception has been used by individual groups of the UCA in the Oakland area and in its recent drive to secure wider political influence.[6] The COG have used young women members in England to sexually seduce prospective members ("flirty fishing"). Bromley and Shupe compared the recruiting techniques used by the Oakland Family in its recruiting for the UCA with those of the Billy Graham Evangelical Association, which orchestrate similar group reactions (but perhaps not saturated to the same degree as the Oakland Family). Brainwashing is not at issue, but attempts to influence attitudes are, and those influenced by these NRMs are not turned into zombies or robots. An alternative explanation to brainwashing is given in the next section on *depro-*

gramming. Further, NRM membership numbers tend to be relatively stable, indicating a considerable attrition rate, except perhaps for the Church of Scientology.

Cults are frequently charged with use of violence, but careful study indicates that modern NRMs are more likely to be recipients of violence than initiators. Both NRM and anti-NRM groups have engaged in violence, but with NRMs this seems more likely a reaction to harassment. Deprogrammers have been engaged by parents to kidnap their children from NRMs, a violent, serious offense, but these actions have been inconsistently prosecuted and the deprogrammers sometimes convicted.

Fund-raising by new religions has been strongly criticized, but the practices of typical charities are also far from ideal. Many of the new religions have relatively small needs for money which they meet through small businesses or donations from members. Moonies and Hare Krishnas need more money and sometimes their begging and soliciting is annoying and even harassing. Scientology raises money through sale of lessons, although they may have other businesses as well. Attempts to protect the public from these groups (the cure), would likely be worse than the disease, for even if some or all of these groups are fraudulent, people have a constitutional right to do foolish things.

Deprogramming

"Deprogramming" has gotten a good deal of attention, both from the media and from the anti-cult movement. NRM members are often depicted as zombies under "mind control," but when the deprogrammers' practices are examined,[7] they are attempting to persuade, influence, and reason with the person and to undermine their beliefs. If the member of an NRM was truly under "mind control," such methods would not work. Deprogramming does not work the way it is represented, since there is no brainwashing to begin with. The process is not only without legal support, but potentially dangerous to mental health. The similarity of stories from people after deprogramming springs from the basic ideology and justification of the deprogrammers. One team that has studied this topic asserted "Deprogrammers are self-serving, illegal, and fundamentally immoral. In some cases, despite their protests to the contrary, they have profited handsomely from this practice."[8] The deprogrammer in the CBS presentation on "48 Hours" may have been sincere, but such behavior is nevertheless a violation of civil rights as well as illegal under older statutes.

Deconversion, or exiting from an NRM has a number of paths:

1. *exiting* or voluntary departure, in which the person leaves
   a. *covertly* (without letting others know, and more often an impulsive act likely among newer members),
   b. *overtly* (letting others know quietly, perhaps to prompt some desired change, more likely among longer-term members), or
   c. *declaratively* (clearly stating the reasons).
2. *expulsion* or ejection by the group does occur, but is less common and seems an outcome of leadership struggles, or an effort to get rid of those whose commitment is doubted, to deal with dissidents, rule-breakers, or members who are not able to care for themselves (psychiatric casualties).
3. *extraction* or coercive or noncoercive departure initiated by outside person(s). In *extraction* this seems to generally go better where the family is supportive and available and where the process is noncoercive. Efforts to amend guardianship and conservator statutes in several states were nearly successful at one time, but such legal maneuvers have been overruled on appeal.

Perhaps a third of the persons forcibly deprogrammed return to the New Religious Movements, possibly more confirmed in their faith and less able to leave when they otherwise might wish to. Those whose forcible deprogramming has "taken" are more likely to be involved in the anti-cult movement and to be more vehement in their rejection of their former NRM involvement. Coercive deprogramming may be declining, partly for legal reasons and partly because the most visible "destructive cults" (Moonies, Krishnas) have had a recruiting decline.[9]

People who leave after a noncoercive reevaluation in which they are persuaded to reconsider their views rarely have horror stories to tell, but those who leave after coercive deprogramming will sometimes recount atrocity stories (which may have some truth to them). These legitimize the person's return to the family and justify the expense and possibly illegal actions of the parents. Those former members who merely left had more balanced and less intense attitudes toward the former group and were less involved in the anti-cult movement.

Joining a New Religious Movement—Between Parents and Child

Many parents more or less reluctantly accept their children's decisions; some attempt to argue or discuss the matter with their children, while a few are so angry, offended, or opposed that they undertake radical action, such as hiring coercive deprogrammers. At one conference Bromley and Shupe[10] noted that these parents were all quite well-to-do or held prestigious or substantial positions. They remarked that parents have to consider that they have failed as parents, have defective children, or that the NRMs have "brainwashed" their children.

Bromley and Shupe suggested that this conflict between parents and child is a clash of interests rather than a form of mental health therapy. Nevertheless, the dialogues Bromley and Shupe described between parent and child and those on the "48 Hours"[11] show are similar to family therapy. Parents see their hopes and plans for their children disrupted, their children no longer emotionally responsive or amenable to parental influence, perhaps not even physically available, and hopes for grandchildren imperiled. The primary conflict seems to be between parents and children, as the new religions do not really affect the interests of either the government or the churches. Bromley and Shupe concluded:

> Parents are correct in their assessment that converts to the new religions are turning their backs on their pasts as well as on previous plans for the future. These youth may indeed come to regret their naiveté and exuberance in later years . . . But the converts are quite correct in *their* contention that they are adults, however inexperienced in long-range decision-making, and therefore possess the right to chart their own courses in life. The real irony is that in most instances the conflict does not persist. Left to their quests, most converts to the new religions ultimately drop out and resume their former lives . . . The possibility for family reconciliation increases with the passage of time.[12]

I might add that from my experience converts will likely renew their family ties if the families have not made this impossible. NRMs may be regarded as opportunities for young adults to:

1. grow up and separate from their families,
2. repair earlier losses through a committed set of relationships,
3. provide meaning to their lives, or
4. get off drugs and acquire skills they missed out on.

The current charges against NRMs are indistinguishable from those leveled against other new religions, including the Roman Catholic church, Quakers, Jehovah's Witnesses, Christian Scientists, Mennonites, and Mormons. While some of the NRMs engage in deceptive practices and questionable recruiting practices, governmental intrusion is sufficiently risky that mainline churches, which were most affected by membership losses, have not demanded it. Such intrusion hardens the NRMs' position, making it harder for members to leave and it reduces diversity and damages democracy; a danger and loss to all.[13] Finally, some new religions grow up to become the new mainline churches.

Satanic "Cults"

Few issues generate more fear among people who have seen a loved one become involved in an NRM than the prospect that the NRM is satanic. A taste for "heavy metal" or "punk rock" music is sometimes equated with Satanism. Before we consider what is involved here, some information and definitions may be helpful. As was noted in chapter 3, Satan comes from the Hebrew *sahtan*, meaning adversary, and was not a name. Thus when *sahtan* gradually became the Satan of Christianity, it relieved people from having to attribute evil to an all-powerful God who was supposed to be all-good. In Jewish thought Satan was never well-established, as Jews considered people to have both a good impulse (*yetzer tov*) and an evil impulse (*yetzer ha-ra*) and the capacity for choice.

The worship of Satan, although sometimes grouped with the occult,[14] is intimately tied to Christianity with its inversion of symbols and rites of the mass. From the appearance of Michael Aquino, founder of the Temple of Set on "The Oprah Winfrey Show" and Geraldo Rivera's show on Satanism one would suppose this is a large, evil movement. A good deal of the material reported in the media as satanic is either mislabeled, nonexistent, or used to deflect attention from ordinary or heinous crimes. Sensational reports of animal and human sacrifices and ritual abuse are mostly not substantiated, or the evidence is ambiguous.[15]

It seems that there are three types of satanic groups: "(1) solitary Satanists, (2) 'outlaw' cults, and (3) neo-Satanic churches."[16] The solitary Satanists are typically alienated, highly disturbed adolescents who concoct their own practices and rituals with little or no connection with others. The outlaw cults seem much the same as the first but with larger numbers, with perhaps a wider range of deviant and harmful behaviors. The recent reports of a group of Mexican drug dealers committing human sacrifices seems in this category. Larger, more coherent groups are the Church of Satan, originated by Anton LaVey in San Francisco in 1966 and the Temple of Set, founded by Michael Aquino and his wife Lillith Sinclair. These rely on LaVey's *The Satanic Bible* and *The Satanic Rituals*, and the principles of both churches advocate power, domination, and indulgence. Both churches are flamboyant, but both prohibit harm to people or animals, sacrifices, or the use of blood in rituals. It is ironic that both LaVey and Aquino have been irritated by the presence of clearly disturbed people attracted to the doctrines or practices of their churches.

The solitary Satanists and "outlaw" cults, on the other hand can be dangerous because "traditional Satanist worship has at its center the evocation of Satan and the Black Mass, which parodies the Roman Catholic rite. It has great emotional intensity and includes strong overtones of ventilation of anger against God and society. Needless to say, Satanism attracts its share of sociopathic persons. . . ."[17]

But Shouldn't Something Be Done?

A person or group engaged in illegal acts such as sexual or ritual abuse of children, or the abuse or sacrifice of animals merits prosecution, for these are serious offenses;

and freedom of religion is not a defense. If however, a group of adults engages in offensive acts (group sex, use of excrement in a Black Mass, reading the Latin Mass backwards, or using an inverted cross or a black host), these are abhorrent but not illegal acts, and the "cure" of suppression risks the religious liberties of all.

Similarly, the heavy metal and punk rock music of the seventies and eighties has generated intense opposition from some parents and fundamentalist Christian groups. They have claimed that these recorded items contain subliminal messages, "backward-masked" (embedded messages played backwards) to prevent discovery. This is a misuse of the term backward masking; the evidence is that audio messages that are recorded backward cannot be decoded unless the tape is also played backward. Heavy metal music may be loud, tasteless, and simple, but the hearing of healthy youngsters seems more at risk than their mental health. It may push an already very disturbed adolescent over the edge, however. Police and parent groups that promote "de-metaling" or other "rehabilitations" are likely secular disguises for fundamentalist views. The fear of a satanic network attempting to destroy American youth has little foundation. What little danger there is comes from loners or small groups of very disturbed people.[18]

It is also worth knowing that competent police agencies, such as state police organizations around the country are definitely interested in reports of satanic groups or cult-type activity. From my contacts with state police officers at the central office level, I know that these matters are of active interest and reports are followed up. There are instances of "outlaw" cults but reports of some wide conspiracy do not lead to hard physical evidence of crime. Either these satanic groups are uniformly more effective in concealing reported murders of large numbers of people from well-trained investigators, or there seems to be less than meets the eye in most satanic churches and groups. A few can be idiosyncratic or dangerous, but these can be dealt with through current laws.

Repeated experience has shown that prohibition increases attractiveness, making such intervention counterproductive.

Nevertheless, this does not mean that there is nothing to do. A person's attraction to a satanic church may well be regarded as:

1. an indication of considerable feelings of isolation, alienation, and rejection of the ordinary values and practices of one's family. In adolescents, this may be no more than an expression of anger or a way to differentiate from the family in a mode most likely to upset the largest number of people. While these interests may signal personal distress, neither panic nor disinterest are best. Family counseling may be a first choice, since the adolescent may be unwilling to be regarded as the sole problem. If the adolescent recognizes the presence of serious personal distress, individual treatment as an adjunct to family counseling is an alternative.

2. the formation of a stable and accepted sense of oneself as evil. This is a malignant development in anyone, implying the risk of damaging behavior with little or no discomfort, shame, or guilt. Thus symptoms or distress that might lead the person to seek professional help might also be absent.[19] Such a person might refuse any help unless in serious trouble with the law.

Illness, Pain, Aging, and Death

Illness, aging, and death are painful, inescapable realities we all encounter as they slash across the human bonds that support us in a web of relationships. Archaeological studies of some of the earliest manifestations of human culture show the presence of ritual burial practices.[20] No other species does this. These early practices suggest both the awareness of death and the effort to memorialize the person as if still living. Tools, art, and burial rites thus seem to characterize the origins of humanity as a self-aware species.

As we discussed in the previous chapter, our capacity to use signs and symbols gives "explanations" power to modify our experiences of events. No wonder our ancestors were deeply impressed with the power of the word,[21] and many words have been devoted to dealing with central issues of existence—birth, life, pain, illness, aging, loss, and death. Related to these is the problem of evil. No concise treatment can do justice to the complexity of these topics, but I will try to provide a framework within which to approach the problems of evil and explanations in counseling, when religious matters are also involved.

It may be useful, but an oversimplification, to suggest a few basic views of the world:

1. the world has meaning and order (and is basically good, or is dangerous and perhaps malicious),
2. the world is random, and
3. the world is controlled by deities that care little for humans, but need to be appeased.

With the rise of science, the last view has ebbed, but this ancient pagan idea may be returning. While concepts of justice and of the interest of the gods in human behavior antedate the monotheism of the Hebrew patriarchs and prophets, the uncompromising ethical monotheism recorded in the Old Testament also incorporated an ancient idea that if something unexpected happened, it was the work of God. Unusual events such as the parting of the Red Sea (actually the Sea of Reeds) and a person's early death are two examples of occurrences attributed to the action of God.

But this left an insoluble problem. Pain and suffering happened to some good people without apparent justification, while some evil people prospered. If God was just, how could this be understood? This is exactly the problem tackled by the Book of Job. The Book of Job seems to really be two books. The opening and closing chapters recount Satan's challenges to God over Job's goodness, the loss of Job's children and possessions, the occurrence of agonizing illnesses, Job's continued faithfulness, and his restoration to children, possessions, and health. The middle chapters were probably added by an immensely thoughtful writer, who used the story to sensitively explore the various answers his society provided to the presence of these miseries juxtaposed with the view of God as all-powerful and all-good. In the middle chapters, Job's friends who "comfort" him present the standard answers. Job is really sinful and getting what he deserves, or he has only behaved well because of the rewards God provided. Finally Job, who never relinquishes his faith in God's goodness and power, calls God to account—and God answers out of the whirlwind (a powerful answer worth re-reading).[22] God does not explain to Job, but confronts him on his limited understanding, and Job withdraws his accusation.

The basic problem in Job has been well posed by Kushner[23] in his book *When Bad Things Happen to Good People*, using three true but conflicting statements. To summarize, he put them as:

A. God is all-powerful and causes everything that happens in the world. Nothing happens without His willing it.
B. God is just and fair, and stands for people getting what they deserve, so that the good prosper and the wicked are punished.
C. Job is a good person.

Logically, when Job suffers, only two of the three statements hold, and the choice is which to drop. Kushner opted to modify statements A and B by proposing that

God tries to make the world fair and just, but cannot always do so. Kushner quotes from Job, chapter 40, in which God tells Job, "*You* tread down the wicked" (p. 43) and then God will acknowledge Job's power. Kushner concluded that while God may not be omnipotent, God is available for support, comfort, and guidance. This conclusion, which is much better elaborated in Kushner's book, may not satisfy everyone.

Bakan's[24] discussion amplifies Kushner's ideas. Bakan proposed that suffering[25] supposes a certain level of awareness, and may be ameliorated either through understanding or forgetfulness. He preferred understanding because it had implications for the modern view of the nature of disease. While many diseases require a specific bacteria, virus, or parasite, other conditions are often needed too. These include various elements in the person's background, including dysfunctional, rejecting families, deficient interpersonal relationships, estrangement, stress, and personality dimensions. Referring to the work of Selye,[26] Bakan paralleled physiological and psychological defenses,[27] showing how both function in automatic ways that can also injure the very person they protect. For both types of defenses, the cure is self-knowledge or understanding.

Self-knowledge should allow people to understand their lives, the quality of their interpersonal relationships, what stresses are being endured, and to face the consequences of their adaptation to these stresses. The very nature of psychological defenses usually precludes this sort of understanding without counseling. To add to a "wish list" of understandings however, some comprehension of death is important. While specific medical treatment has increased overall longevity, maximum longevity seems less affected. Everyone dies.

Bakan briefly reviewed Darwinian concepts related to natural selection. Bakan argued that the common assumption that the characteristics chosen by natural selection favor individual survival is incorrect. Rather, it is necessary for the group to survive, but this may be at the individual's expense. Death, he suggested, is necessary for group survival, and although he did not make this point specific, death provides ways to aid species adaptation by allowing new members to have an opportunity to develop increased adaptability through trying new ways of existence.

Just as Kushner dealt with the Book of Job, so did Bakan. In the Judeo-Christian tradition death is viewed as a punishment from God, which Bakan saw as a basic error because "so conceiving of death perverts the fact that death is inevitable in time and will occur whether the life lived has been virtuous or not. Virtue might be associated with longevity, but it does not provide immortality."[28]

Thus the person for whom God is just, fair, and omnipotent, and who wants a coherent understanding of the world, can no longer see death as God's punishment, but must begin to see it only as an aspect of His world. Death does not contain a "message" to an individual although it may be God's way to allow various species, including humanity, to have their best opportunity to survive—but there are no guarantees to either individuals or species.

"Answers," "Explanations," and Responses

In counseling, clients often want, and even demand answers. An answer can be comforting, if it makes the person's world appear whole again. Kushner's book deals with well-meaning but devastating "answers" freely offered to comfort the bereaved. These, with the real meaning in brackets, include:

1. It was a punishment for sin. [If not the deceased's, then yours.]
2. God needed him more. [You did not love or need him enough; his death is really your fault.]
3. She is now free from pain and in a better world. [You did not make this world nice enough for her.]
4. If only . . . [It's really someone's fault.]

5. Don't cry, he wouldn't want you to. [Don't burden *me* with your pain.]
6. God does not give you a heavier burden than you can carry. [Implies the person's strength caused the pain.]

And there is the classic, "I don't know what to say" [meaning, I cannot bring the deceased back to life]. There are others, but if these answers are destructive, what answers are not?

It is important to recognize that while the dead cannot be revived, the living can be comforted, and their pain can be expressed through one's support and presence. To keep pain inside is damaging in the long run. The counselor can help by not giving meaningless answers, even if it means saying that there are no answers. As well, the living may well be angry at the dead, both for real hurts in their lives together, as well as in angry grief over feeling abandoned by the person who died.

Sometimes the person may express satisfaction or even vindication at the death of a relative. Here, saying "you don't really mean that" is again avoiding the other person's bitterness for one's own comfort, without recognizing the extent of the pain the living must feel and have felt to express such feelings. Empathy (feeling with) is appropriate, even without either condoning or condemning the person in such distress. When people who have lost, or are losing, someone apply these "answers" to themselves, the counselor may have to explore where these ideas have come from, and may intervene by helping to express the underlying meanings to see whether that is what is really intended.

Suicide

Judaism, Christianity, and Islam all oppose suicide. However, all allow for, and even glorify martyrdom[29] which, when the person is presented with a choice (typically conversion), is a form of suicide. Martyrdom is regarded as fidelity to one's faith and may be an affirmation of selfhood. All three religions strongly disapprove of, and apply sanctions to the suicide; although in Judaism and Christianity at least, increased psychological awareness has led to expanded latitude in allowing for the loss of free will when a person chooses self-destruction. In this country, increased latitude is likely in the Islamic community too.

While a strong religious affiliation is likely to reduce the risk of suicide somewhat, the risk is never zero. Risk factors include being older, unmarried, in poor physical health, unemployed or retired, from a broken home, living alone, making infrequent use of health agencies, having severe emotional difficulties, membership in certain groups, and prior history of suicide attempts. Men and women differ in regard to suicidal potential—women are three times as likely as men to attempt suicide; men are three times as likely to succeed. Adolescents are more frequently at risk than mature adults, but there is an increasing recognition that preadolescent children do make suicide threats and can sometimes execute them. I know of at least one suicidal gesture by an eight-year-old boy, but frequently such behavior is not recognized for what it is by adults. Elderly adults are also at increased risk when health and finances decline and important relationships are lost.

Certain factors tend to reduce suicide potential. While age, gender, ethnic membership, and past history are fixed elements, employment and financial status can sometimes be improved. Quality and quantity of relationships can be enhanced, as can health under certain circumstances. In brief, suicide is affected by relationships, which points to one avenue of intervention. Where a client presents as, or is thought to be, at risk for depression, part of the interview should be aimed at evaluating suicidal potential. Even children can be asked.

There are a number of myths about suicide that interfere with effective coping by professionals. First it must be recognized that it is a very intimidating experience even for very experienced professionals if a client threatens suicide, or gives indications of suicidal potential. Counselors may fend off this kind of fear by saying:

	Myth	*Reality*
1.	"This is just a bid for attention," (meaning—if I ignore it, it will go away).	While suicidal threats can be manipulative, it is a desperate move.
2.	"People who talk about suicide do not follow through," (meaning—this is not too serious).	Most (80 percent) suicides give indications of this intent.
3.	"Suicide is a sick, irrational act," (meaning—it is unpredictable so I have no control).	Suicidal people may be very unhappy, but not necessarily psychotic.
4.	"If the client starts to improve, the crisis is over," (meaning—I don't have to worry now).	More energy, especially in the absence of good reason, is cause for real worry.
5.	"A suicidal person can't change," (meaning—there is nothing I can do, so why try).	Suicide is frequently a temporary state of mind.[30]

There are certain issues to explore if depression or suicide is suspected.

1. Inquire if the client is depressed (unless he or she has already declared this), and if so, how badly does he or she feel.
2. Explore suicide in a way the client can understand (do you sometimes want to hurt yourself? or, do you some-

times wish you would sleep and never wake up? or, do you sometimes think of killing yourself?).
3. If there is an affirmative response, even if the client states a "no," query the person about their thoughts about doing this, and how long they have been contemplating this step.
4. Try to find out whether the client has a previous history of suicidal thoughts and/or suicide attempts.
5. If the client has made plans, or even indicates clear awareness of available means, try to get the details.
6. If the client indicates possession of the necessary materials, try to see if the client will surrender them to you.

In instances 5. and 6. there is clear suicidal risk, and it may also be present in 4. Immediate intervention should be *considered*. This does not mean you should panic, but if this is a new client, then the client's attachment to you is likely to be slim and the risk is higher. Even if the client presents with another problem, serious suicidal potential nearly always overrides other considerations. If possible, the situation needs to be explored in some detail, considering both facts and feelings. The counselor also needs to try to make an emotional connection with the client in *this* session, as this sort of link is likely to reduce the prospect of an immediate act.

Sometimes questions such as those above are objected to because they will "give people ideas." The only ideas such questions give to clients is that the person talking to them takes them seriously, is not afraid of their pain or anger, and may actually be interested in them, all of which operate to build a connection with the client, which reduces the risk of suicide.

People who are intent on suicide are frequently angry at someone, and this is likely to include the counselor if they have had a few sessions. Suicide is frequently an aggressive act and the counselor has to look for the anger and deal with it directly. Even when others deserve the greater anger, I find it useful to firmly suggest the client is angry with me, and to try to find something I have done that could have elicited some anger. From there, we can go on to the sources of greater pain to the client. While taking suicide seriously, I may also say, "Suicide is a permanent answer to a temporary problem" (if this is reasonably the case, as it often is with adolescents). I do what I can to ventilate at least some anger and develop as much of a relationship as I can at that point. This can include offering several firm appointments, if they have not already been set, trying to elicit a promise from the client not to do anything before the next session, and making sure the client knows how to reach me between sessions, and knows that he or she can. Some professionals require a formal, written no-suicide contract, but I prefer to let clients feel that I trust their word. I will ask if the client feels a need to enter a hospital if the depression is deep or the intent is strong, but I try to assess whether I am responding to the client's distress or mine. A hospital is a last resort and it is better for the idea to come from the client.

But these milder interventions may not work. The client may be very, very angry at the counselor. If there is a reality to that anger, an apology is due the client and quite worthwhile. I may also say that I want to continue to work with the client but can not do that if the client is dead. Very troubled people may be using anger to punish the counselor, so I may say, "If you kill yourself, I can't see you any more. I'll get another client, but you won't have another therapist."[31]

If the client is an elderly person with a terminal illness, and in pain, suggesting that suicide is irrational or hurtful to others is lacking in simple humanity. Considering how the client can make something of whatever time is left may be much kinder, especially with the availability of the Hospice movement and effective pain medication.

As an example of how one can overlook the risks involved when a client is not explicit, I had one client in whom I did not recognize the degree of her depression. During a holiday period, she was alone. Although she rarely drank, she began to drink on an empty stomach from a bottle of whiskey she had received as a gift. Her roommate returned home unexpectedly early, to find her unconscious and in respiratory distress. A prompt call to the hospital led to emergency intervention that probably saved her life. She was not consciously aware of her wish to die so this is an atypical example of suicide, but it does illustrate the complexity of the assessment of suicidal risk and the need to be aware of the possibility when depression is present.

Finally, it should be noted that the counselor's appeal to religious prohibitions is a desperate intervention. Suicide seems to be largely, but perhaps not completely, independent of religious affiliation in this country, although there are some differences among groups as a function of age, gender, and ethnic membership.

But Isn't This a Manipulation?

Counselors and therapists are often worried about manipulative clients, which is somehow a "bad" thing. We call people manipulators if they are better at it than we are.[32] We seem worried that clients will get something they don't deserve. Actually if clients felt they had a better route to getting what they want, they would take it; and if they could, they might not need to be our clients. That clients feel the counselor is *worth* manipulating means we have a better opportunity to connect with them and help them with their problems.

While taking suicidal thoughts or threats seriously, particularly when they first appear, it is also important neither to panic (because this frightens clients), nor to dismiss these thoughts as unimportant or manipulative. To do the latter can provoke clients to "prove" themselves or to leave.

Some clients add to their distress by talking of how great a sin they are contemplating or what a slap at God suicide is. These feelings are important to explore rather than debate theologically. The client who sees suicide as an offense or slap at God is likely, in part, to be angry at God. These feelings must be explored in a framework that conveys that God can tolerate the client's anger and does not strike back for anger—but someone in the client's life probably did. As for suicide being a sin, most counselors would agree it is, if the original meaning is used—an error.

5

Counseling, Collaboration, and Referral

The Initial Phase of Counseling

By the time a client has made the first contact with the counselor or agency, he or she has experienced a great deal of pain and frustration, has received a good deal of advice, suggestions, and even directions (which usually have not worked), and now feels desperation and perhaps despair. The counselor, and perhaps there were others in the past, is now regarded as a last resort, a sign of the client's failure in managing the ordinary matters of life. The client may have little hope, but much doubt. Clients may want assurance in this very first contact and counselors may want to offer it. The problem is how. I find it most useful to begin by asking "What seems to be the problem?" or "What seems to be the trouble?" This works even with clients who are themselves counselors. Clients who have already had contact with some part of the mental health system have likely found that the interviewer may have another agenda; making a diagnosis or getting a GAS (Global Assessment Scale) rating for the agency's statistics. By beginning where the client is, the counselor is implicitly saying "I want to work on *your* problem, not mine."

The Reluctant Client

Not all clients come willingly. Children and adolescents are often brought because they are a problem to someone else; parent, teacher, principal, court, or police. Some clients come because an employer or spouse has threatened firing or divorce. If the client *can* recognize the need to come, then while you may have to deal with resentment toward you or the person exerting pressure, the client can begin. When the person identified as the client does not accept this status, this has to be explored. The designated client may not really be the right person. In one instance, a woman in her mid-twenties presented her child of two and one-half for treatment because of her conflict with the child. Separated from her husband for the third time, she was unable to complete the separation and divorce she wanted. She was able to begin to look at her own issues even though her child was the initial topic of discussion for several interviews.

Religious Differences and Similarities

Because there are so many religious options in this country, including "none," the chances are good that the counselor and client will differ in religious orientation. It is daunting when a client challenges the counselor's status on personal salvation. If at all possible, the counselor should try to explore the meanings of this question. Are you totally reliable? or Are you identical with me? or Will you judge me with the same severity (or charity) as my pastor? are some possible meanings. The question "Are you a Christian?" can have more than one meaning. It may mean, Are you a member of a church? or Were you baptized? or Are you Catholic[1] or Protestant? or Have you been saved (converted)? Counselors who were baptized and are members of a church are nevertheless frequently not regarded as saved, or even Christian in this last sense, because they "have not accepted Jesus as their personal Savior," so the counselor may need to inquire first before answering.

The client's need for total trust at the start of counseling may indicate complicating factors, including a fragile sense of self, a history of abuse, or great difficulty in tolerating ambiguity. If a client accepts assurances without qualm, this may connote considerable desperation, which also puts the counseling process at later risk from the ordinary disappointments and failures inherent to counseling. Similarly, the wish for the counselor and client to be identical indicates a poorly organized sense of self and/or difficulty in emotional connections with others. Thus, whether or not counselors regard themselves as saved, exploring the meanings is desirable.

In the absence of a direct question, offering information about the counselor's religious or spiritual state when the topic of religious affiliation is brought up is sometimes considered a sign of counselor openness. Without a clear understanding of the meaning of such information to the client, offering it may burden a client with unwished-for knowledge. But if the client inquires, and the question has been explored, a direct answer is preferable to an evasion.[2]

If the counselor and client share the same religious orientation, this may assist the initial connection. The counselor can be seen as understanding many things without elaborate explanation. By the same token, the counselor may assume an understanding when, in fact, the client intends an individual meaning. Sometimes a person with a religious orientation may choose a counselor for similarities in background, yet not bring religious issues into counseling to any substantial degree.[3]

A counselor with a different religious background needs to be aware of not knowing many things, and to be ready to be educated. My own introduction to this topic began many years ago when I was working with a young woman with a strong, but conflicted Catholic background. Recognizing that I did not know much of what she had experienced, I asked for some material and she gave me *Father Connell's "The New Baltimore Catechism"* to read. Now much out of date since its publication in 1941, it was nevertheless influential in her life and helped me to grasp some of her experiences.

Preparation for Counseling

Some clients expect advice, moral persuasion and even direction of their lives, while others are more sophisticated and understand that counseling helps them to find their own answers. For most people however, some statement of how to proceed is helpful. Starting with "What seems to be the problem?" or "What seems to be the trouble?" is a useful opening. After I have heard what the client understands of the problem, I may reply with a summary of my understanding of what they have said and, if that is correct, perhaps ask for clarification or further information. If I do not feel the need for clarification at that point, I will just encourage the client to continue. If the client seems uncertain of what to do, or asks how this will help, I say that I need to know a good deal about the situation the client is in and he or she can tell me whatever comes to mind since it is probably all connected anyhow.

If the client asks for advice, I do not say that I will not give advice or that it won't help them, but rather, I may say, "You have probably already received a lifetime supply of advice and if it worked then you wouldn't be here now. So let's try to understand your situation and see what we can make of it." Many clients will laugh and admit that this is true. While on this topic, it is important to remember that most advice is given as an accusation. "Why don't you . . .?" This is almost always a put-down. If, in talking with a client about a situation, I see a reasonable course of action that I think the client might well have considered, I might ask "What do you suppose would happen if you. . .?" which opens up the topic of what is getting in the client's way rather than suggesting a course of action. If the client jumps at the idea, I slow the client down and ask that it be explored.

Sometimes after exploring a problem with clients, they may let me know in a later session that they have taken my advice (which I never offered). If I ask, clients will acknowledge that I really did not tell them what to do, but they felt the understanding they developed was like advice.

But Why Isn't Prayer (or Faith) Enough?

This question is often uncomfortable to handle since the counselor may feel that an answer may seem a challenge to the client's faith and lose the client. Here an explanation of the way in which people are able to learn may be helpful. What makes it possible for humans to learn as much as they do is that they have fewer "hard wired" patterns than are found in most other species. Thus they have to learn a great deal, and once a problem is encountered and an effective way of dealing with it is found, this solution becomes automatic.[4] When the situation changes, as situations often do, the automatic patterns or solutions tend to persist. Counseling helps the person become more aware of the original problem and the original solution, and the client can more readily adopt new solutions. There is nothing wrong with prayer, but it is a deliberate act and does not deal well with automatic patterns of feelings, attitudes, and behavior. If the client persists in insisting that prayer *should* help with the problem, then the meaning of prayer needs to be explored.

The Early Appraisal of Client Difficulties

Many counselors feel that their goal is to accept and understand the client from within his or her own world and not to impose outside values, judgments, or views.[5] This is sometimes taken to mean that the counselor should make no appraisal about the utility, effectiveness, or adaptiveness of the client's behaviors, feelings, or attitudes. If such an appraisal makes no difference in what the counselor does, then I would agree. But counselors can do different things which can aid or hinder progress in counseling, and one useful step is to try to understand whether the person's religious orientation and practices are relatively adaptive, or more related to individual emotional problems.

Many clients are reluctant to disclose their religious experiences or attitudes until they have tested the counselor with "small stuff," or asked several indirect questions. The counselor should welcome the client's expression of distrust as a precursor to deeper involvement in counseling. If the client begins to recount personal religious experiences, it is important to try to set these experiences into the context of the person's childhood denomination as well as the current religious group. Thus, speaking in tongues (glossolalia) is an accepted expression in many Pentecostal churches, but is most unusual in a United Methodist congregation. If a client was Methodist but practiced glossolalia, a counselor would probably want to think about the client's emotional integrity.

Based on several sources,[6] including personal experience, I find the following characteristics suggest that the client may be using religious expression mainly to help deal with emotional problems.

1. *Self-oriented display*: Exhibition or boasting of one's good deeds, piety, charity, etc.
2. *Religion as reward*: Expecting, and even demanding that the world (or God) should treat the client well, based on good behavior, good thoughts, or piety.
3. *Scrupulosity*: A persistent concern for one's sinfulness and an overriding preoccupation with never doing anything

that could ever be construed as wrong or sinful. Sometimes carried to the point that the client actually does hurt others, there may also be the underlying pride of being the worst sinner of all.

4. *Relinquishing responsibility*: Saying "the Devil made me do it," or "we are all sinners" to evade localizing accountability for the client's behavior, or the behavior of someone in the client's life.
5. *Ecstasy or frenzy*: While also a feature in some churches, a personal ecstasy may express early emotional deprivation and an intense effort to restore a sense of personal wholeness and vitality.
6. *Recurrent church-changing*: Although changing the church attended is partly determined by what churches are available, the persistent inability to find a congregation to connect with (assuming the person does not change vicinities) may signal particular difficulties in holding onto relationships.
7. *Indiscriminate attitudes*: No religion or church is perfect in all things and for everyone. The client whose enthusiastic and indiscriminate attitude persists for an extended time is expressing a response more typical of childhood.
8. *Doubled-sided "love"*: Far from being a simple emotion, love can also be a vehicle for some quite different feelings or intents, including anger, dependency, and immaturity. If someone in the client's life declares love, the behaviors that follow and the feelings that develop are often a better guide to intention than the verbal statement.
9. *The Bible as a guide to everything*: The Bible is a complex text spanning some two millennia, and challenging some of the world's best minds with its subtleties, silences, indirections, and ambiguities. The narratives have a special charm and insight into complex relations among people, and between people and their God. Finding in it a moment-to-moment guide to all of the daily choices and problems in this existence suggests the client is adopting another form of relinquishing responsibility. Further, the person may be looking to deal with the real insecurities and dangers endured earlier in life.
10. *Possession*: I have only worked with one client who felt

> that the Devil spoke to him, and that he saw the Devil. He feared for the Devil's possession of his soul, and after a while for my soul too. Where a client feels he or she has been possessed, and where apparent personality changes appear, then very serious personality distortions are indicated and the counselor may want to think of multiple personality disorder or borderline personality disorder. A consultation is definitely indicated unless the counselor is well experienced with these problems.

Not all religious expression reflects dysfunction. Some aspects are positive and show creative coping with life's problems. Based on several sources,[7] including personal experience, the following suggest a more adaptive use of religion.

1. *Awareness of complexity*: Religious problems and writings are often complex, and an awareness of their multi-faceted nature suggests a maturity of intellectual and emotional development.
2. *Willingness to try alternatives*: The religion of the client's parents may be a suitable channel for religious expression, but if the client has experimented, the selection made is more likely to issue from a mature choice.
3. *"Conversion"*: This is related to number 2 and does not refer to the usual meaning, but only that the client went through a period of struggle before coming to a resolution.
4. *Coherence*: While all religions have complexities with competing, but not necessarily consistent directives, the adherent's task is to organize, select, and live his or her life in accord with some coherent picture. The client who extols the virtues of love but is brutal in disciplining his or her children is not displaying coherence.
5. *Stability*: All religions have expectations of their adherents, and some are inconvenient or difficult to implement. Stability implies that when the client falls short of these expectations, this will be experienced as an indication of the

need for effort, rather than an easy adjustment of values to meet the current level of behavior, or attitude.

6. *Respect for boundaries*: A religious affiliation may carry with it a good deal of enthusiasm and willingness to work to promote the client's religious ideals. In a multi-religious society such as this, there are limits beyond which a person's enthusiasm at proselytizing is considered intrusive. While appraising this is certainly a matter for the counselor's judgment, a teacher in a secularly based educational setting who persists in attempting to teach his or her religion (rather than teaching about religions) has well overstepped the boundaries.

In the initial phase, the counselor will develop a preliminary sense of the client's difficulties. Seriously distorted religious ideas or practices are quite likely to be accompanied by a similar degree of difficulties in living in other areas of life.

More importantly, the specific configuration of the client's religious ideas and experiences will suggest clues to formative emotional experiences that are now given expression in the religious life of the client. For example, one client believed in God but regarded Him as distant and uninvolved—exactly as she had felt her parents to be while she was growing up. Another client's religious life was bound up primarily with God (the Father) while Jesus (the Son) was relatively not important. Again this paralleled her intense involvement with her father while her younger brother was not significant in her life.

Specific Counseling Approaches with Religious Themes

When religious contents or themes appear, the counselor will need to decide whether anything needs to be done. A client who is expressing some feelings about an experience or person involved in the client's religious life may just be letting the counselor hear about ongoing events. The counselor needs to grasp the degree to which the event or person is particularly important. When it appears that some significant issue is being dealt with, then some of the following approaches may help.

Possibilities in Translations

Muhammad forbade translation of the Qur'an, perhaps understanding the dangers of translation. Nevertheless both the Old and New Testaments have been translated many times, as has the Qur'an; but if two modern translations of the same text are compared, there are nearly always differences. Scholarship has by no means exhausted the possibilities for new understandings of the Bible. Sometimes earlier, and presumably more accurate texts are found, or new translations of obscure words or phrases are offered. Archaeological studies may also shed new light on texts already thought to be understood.

If a client has a particular issue that centers around a specific text or set of texts, the counselor may find it useful to compare several translations of the same material. Consulting a Bible commentary may also help expand the counselor's awareness of the complex meanings embedded in a single word or phrase. Such comparisons are not so likely to be persuasive to a client unless the counselor has first explored what the personal meanings are. For example, there are statements in Proverbs and Ecclesiasticus that advocate physical discipline of children. This was discussed in chapter 3, but here we may see that just presenting that argument to a client whose child discipline seems too severe, or even abusive, probably will not work. The client's feelings, attitudes, and past experiences need to be explored first. If some partial resolution of the emotional bases for the client's adherence to this particular part of the Bible can be achieved, the client may then be able to hear an alternative reading of the Bible text if it is presented in a non-argumentative way.

Paradoxes and Contradictions

Paradoxes and contradictions cause most of us some discomfort. We like the world to be orderly and coherent and when it isn't, we usually try to make it so. One psychologist built a major reputation on this simple fact, although he labeled it "cognitive dissonance." The effort to make one's world coherent can be of use in counseling although the use of contradictions can have negative effects if not employed cautiously. If the client uses the Bible to justify his or her feelings, ideas, or attitudes, then a relatively direct approach can respond to the client by showing an opposing statement in the Bible.[8] Some examples and problems are:

1. *Self-worth.* Psalms 8:5 and Mark 2:27 give examples that deal with human worth, as can a reading of Ecclesiastes 7:16. This has also been succinctly stated as "God doesn't make junk." Depression and rejection of positive feelings or ordinary pleasures runs counter to Proverbs 15:13 and 17:22, Ecclesiastes 8:15, Psalms 30:5, and Luke 15:23.

A useful tool to help find other relevant statements is a concordance. This is a book that allows one to find specific material in the Bible, functioning as a sort of index. I find that an analytical concordance, such as *Young's Analytical Concordance to the Bible*[9] is most useful because it also gives the Hebrew or Greek word in question; but there are many others that are set up in different ways.

2. *Anger.* The expression of anger is a difficult problem for most people. When given a religious coloration, it is that much harder. One of the common justifications opposing the expression of anger is Jesus's injunction to "love your neighbor." What many people *now* do not realize is that Jesus was referring to Leviticus 19:17–18, al-

though his hearers *then* surely knew this. What this says (*The Jerusalem Bible*) is:

> You must not bear hatred for your brother in your heart [i.e. the mind]. You must openly tell him, your neighbour, of his offence; this way you will not take a sin upon yourself. You must not exact vengeance, nor must you bear a grudge against the children of your people. You must love your neighbour as yourself.[10]

A somewhat different translation is found in the *New English Bible*.

> You shall not nurse hatred against your brother. You shall reprove your fellow-countryman frankly and so you will have no share in his guilt. You shall not seek revenge, or cherish anger towards your kinsfolk; you shall love your neighbour as a man like yourself.

What is clear is that the sin described here is to be *silent* when you are angry over another's misdeeds. Similar material is found in Mark 11:15–17 or Matthew 21:12–13, when Jesus threw the money changers out of the Temple, or in John 18:19–24. In Ephesians 4:25–27, allowing anger to fester unresolved was disapproved of by St. Paul. Moses got angry with God (Numbers 11:10–15) and the Hebrews (Exodus 32:1–20), as did Jonah. While not angry, Abraham was politely but persistently argumentative with God in Genesis 18:16–33 over God's plan to destroy Sodom and Gomorrah. In none of these, or other areas, was anger toward God punished.

3. *Alcohol.* The dangers of alcoholism were freely recognized in the Bible, but alcohol (wine and beer) was clearly accepted, *in moderation*, as seen in Psalms 104:15, I Timothy 5:23, 2 Samuel 16:1–4, and other places.

4. *Sex.* The pursuit of sexual pleasure was recognized as capable of causing great injury. However it was not

rejected, but recognized as a basis for the bond between wife and husband, as in Ecclesiastes 9:9. The Song of Songs seems to have been erotic wedding poetry that was allegorically interpreted as the relationship between God and His people. A plain reading, however, shows that love had a physical side that was joyfully accepted. In the New Testament, when there are statements that seem to say that sex or marriage are to be avoided, this was based on the assumption that the world was ending *soon*! Long-term plans would be futile.

These will not deal with all problems, and not all problems will respond to such an approach. Arguing Bible verses with a client rarely works, nor does the person gain any further self-understanding or self-acceptance. It is important to first try to help clients explore their feelings and attitudes before giving alternatives, or the counselor runs the risk of being perceived as the client's enemy.

Forgiveness

Judaism, Christianity, and Islam all see humans as error-prone, if not sinful, and all provide modes for reconciliation and repentance. Forgiveness, generosity, charity, and mercy are common themes. This sometimes comes to mean that if a person has been harmed by another, then forgiveness is a necessity. In some instances, adults who have been sexually and/or physically abused as children are told that if they are to be healed of these injuries, they must forgive the parental or adult abusers.[11] Perhaps it may work sometimes, but I have not found that to be the case. While reconciliation may be a desirable outcome, psychologically, forgiveness has to be earned. To forgive people who do not acknowledge the injury, or even worse, rationalize their injurious behavior as having been deserved, is to sustain the injury all over again. Before the anger, and even hatred can be discharged and dissolved, it must be recalled, felt, expressed (at least to the counselor),[12] and accepted as a valid response to the injury.

Library Aids

Some counselors find written materials quite useful, and these are often employed in vocational or educational counseling where the client may need to acquire specific information. A similar approach can sometimes be of value with religious clients whose understanding of their own religious experiences and training stopped in adolescence, or for those who have continued but who are stuck on some point, or for those who retain only a child-based view of the Bible (which they reject), but want something more. There are a variety of helpful sources for the counselor and some may be usable directly by the client.[13]

Consulting and Collaborating with Clergy

The function of clergy in counseling is ancient, but has been relinquished to a secular profession to a considerable degree in this century. Many people who are impelled to seek counseling regard this as a personal failure and this attitude is intensified for many religious people, who may see the need for counseling as a failure of faith as well. However some congregants will see their pastor, priest or rabbi as safer because of a shared value system,[14] and because they may shore up their religious doubts. Other parishioners may be very reluctant to bring common problems to their clergy, and this seems more likely when the person is a member of a stricter, more conservative denomination.[15]

Still, it appears that clergy are quite likely to be consulted by many people in distress, and the degree to which clergy are willing to undertake such work depends on preference and training, but not age or experience. At some point the priest, pastor or rabbi may see that the problem being presented exceeds the scope of their skills, training, or emotional strength and will want to refer to a professional counselor. At this point, many clergy experience a sense of failure rather than seeing a referral as a responsible professional act. If the clergy does not know the counselor well, the situation is ripe for defensiveness and communication problems.[16] Further, there may not be a clear idea of what counselors do and, among some more conservative clergy there is the suspicion that secular counselors are anti-religion or pro-indulgence. The counselor needs to be sensitive to these land-mines and to explain the counseling process and the purposes of counseling neutrality.

Another potential problem exists regarding confidentiality. While there have been cases of clergy sued for breaches of confidentiality, some clergy feel they should know much or all of what goes on in the counseling of the congregational member they have referred. The counselor has to define and explain the reasons for confidentiality, as well as find appropriate functions for the clergy to continue to fulfill, making it clear that the counselor can not and will not do that which is the province of the pastor. One role for clergy is to consult with the counselor regarding the basic tenets and practices of the client's denomination. Some clients may have distorted or misunderstood their own denomination's central beliefs or practices, or may not know the range of what is possible or permissible. If the counselor is not personally knowledgeable, then the counselor must consult with the minister.

Conflicts in Values

Many clergy are quite accepting of the role and functions of the counselor. For some, there are conflicts in values that are hard to negotiate. Such denominational values as control, obedience, community and parental authority can clash with such counselor values as freedom, pleasure,[17] individuality, and child development.[18] Independent inquiry or curiosity can collide with established denominational doctrines about the importance of belief or not disturbing the faith of other parishioners. When the counselor becomes aware of a value conflict, it is useful to try to discuss this with the pastor, attempting to see matters from the other perspective. Usually it is possible to see that both counselor and clergy have similar enough goals so that collaboration can be fruitful. If the counselor does not set up the goal of winning, the discussion process itself can demonstrate the value of open-ended exploration as a conflict resolution method.

There may be instances when core values and procedures in counseling are under pressure, such as confidentiality, objectivity, or honesty. Occasionally, the counselor may come to conclude that the pastor is, in fact, corrupt, dishonest, or exploitative to a serious degree. This can pose a very serious problem and while I can offer no general solutions, this difficulty has to be faced. Consultation with more experienced colleagues is usually desirable, and sometimes making written records, with the counselor keeping an extra copy. Such precautions are appropriate in any circumstance where this sort of problem is suspected.

Clergy as Clients

Like any other human, clergy "suffer the slings and arrows" of life. While many people will take their own ordinary shortcomings as "only human," to need professional help is often seen as a real failure. Clergy are expected, and often expect themselves, to have neither shortcomings nor the need for professional help—yet sometimes they will need it. If the counselor is approached to provide such assistance, there are certain additional pitfalls to be aware of. Here denominational differences produce considerable variations in the nature of the issues.

For Jews, the rabbinate has a long tradition of being an "amateur" vocation, in that one was forbidden to be paid for work as a rabbi.[19] However, a few hundred years ago it became necessary to compensate such people for the time taken away from other occupations. Today many orthodox Jewish men are ordained rabbis, but work at secular occupations without feeling the need for a congregational appointment.[20] While doubt may be a distressing element in a rabbi's life, greater difficulties are likely to occur in ordinary human relationships, or in the degree to which the rabbi is in conflict about following the detailed behavioral practices of his or her division (Orthodox, Conservative, Reform) within Judaism.

For Christians, doubt is doubly difficult for clergy who may feel they have "betrayed a sacred commitment," particularly if they question their calling.[21] Intense shame is likely to occur too, compounding the person's difficulty and making the minister more likely to withdraw from others who might be helpful. Protestant clergy come from a very diverse spectrum of denominations, so generalizations need caution, but frequently one problem has to do with anger and conflict. These feelings tend to be suppressed, as do sexual thoughts or impulses outside the bounds defined by the church.[22] Specific problem areas can include alcohol use, dependency, and problems with children,[23] among others.

Since clergy are often held up as ideals, as well as severely criticized, the stresses are considerable. It may be hard for ministers to recognize their emotional vulnerability to these stressors. As well, those who are personally emotionally attractive ("charismatic" in the usual sense) may not have enough restraint over impulses. Finally, since the minister is held to have received a "call," this is sometimes an excuse for the congregation to pay a less-than-adequate salary. For someone who has a calling, to bargain about money is often demeaning and very hard to do. Resentment, often without adequate means for resolution, is a common result. While some denominations assign ministers, and rotate them too, others leave the hiring, salary, and firing in the hands of the congregation. This instability in the minister's life also adds stress. Some denominations provide both medical and psychological services for clergy, so the counselor is more likely to see someone for whom those services are not available, or a minister reluctant to seek ordinarily available sources of help, because of the nature of the problem.

The decision and training for the priesthood leads to a self-image as specially chosen,[24] perhaps to a greater degree than is seen with most Protestant clergy. Further, the training for celibacy tends to mute or suppress not only sexual needs, but needs for closeness and affection. One may not see a priest in counseling unless there is no professional help available within the diocese, although an ex-priest or ex-nun is more likely to request counseling. It has been suggested[25] that marital problems are a risk for ex-priests because of difficulties in expressing feelings in an intimate relationship or because of difficulties in one or both partners in adjusting to dramatically different roles.

In addition to the difficulties sketched here, the counselor will also have to deal with his or her own feelings toward the person who is, or was a priest, minister, or rabbi. These include:

1. The client and counselor have different religious orientations.
2. The counselor may still retain some childhood awe of a "man of the cloth," producing a reluctance to take up the client's ordinary human problems, particularly if they share the same denomination.
3. Seeing the human failings of the client, the counselor may react with more anger and rejection, perhaps repeating

the same rejecting experience the counselor experienced as a child.

4. The counselor may personally regard religion as nonsense, to be tolerated in immature people, but not to be inflicted on defenseless children, with the client taking the brunt of the counselor's anger and disapproval.
5. The counselor may be intrigued by the possibility of intellectual discussions, which can impede the ordinary work of counseling.
6. The client may find it particularly difficult to give up the role of being the help*er* and accept being the help*ee*.

Clergy as Counselors

The position of the minister, rabbi, or priest may lend a certain initial advantage or disadvantage to the counseling process, but this quickly comes to depend largely on the personal skills and knowledge of the pastoral counselor. However, an advantage is that for many people clergy are more approachable. As counselors, clergy know more about the specific details of their denominational beliefs and practices, and about the exceptions that exist but are not widely known. A drawback is that many people expect moral judgments to be made about them and may be reluctant to bring up central problems. As well, some clients who choose a therapist with a similar religious orientation yet may not bring religious issues into their therapy.[26] Further, there is some data suggesting that clients are less disclosing when the counselor makes his or her religious orientation known.[27] This has not been my experience when it has come up after a client request for information, but may occur if the information is injected or displayed[28] in an artificial manner.

When and How to Refer

Human problems can be very diverse and no one can handle everything. What is important is to recognize that certain problems exceed one's range of skills and to:

1. secure advice and consultation on how to continue,
2. refer the person, either for help with a specific concern while the counselor continues to work, or to
3. send the client to another professional.

Referral for Ancillary Services

While working with one client who had communication problems with her husband, I had occasion to see the husband and recognized he had serious communication problems that seemed neurologically based. I referred the client's husband for a neurological and neuropsychological evaluation, which confirmed my suspicion. Sometimes children whose parents or teachers complain of their not listening or "only listening when they want to," suffer from recurrent ear infections or a Central Auditory Processing problem. Medical exams and a hearing, and perhaps a Central Auditory Processing evaluation are indicated. When I see a child or adolescent in whom enuresis is a presenting symptom, I ask for a medical evaluation if one has not been done recently. It does not happen often, but sometimes there are medical causes which, when treated, clear up the problem.

Clients may be taking a number of medications that need regular medical supervision. Lithium is a common treatment for manic-depressive conditions, but the therapeutic dose is close to a toxic dose. Regular medical supervision of lithium blood levels is very important. People on long-term psychoactive drugs (major tranquilizers or so-called anti-psychotic drugs) are at serious risk for an irreversible movement disorder called *tardive dyskinesia*. The use of such drugs needs to be reevaluated carefully and regularly. While the physical danger of anorexia is obvious, bulimia (binging and purging through vomiting and/or laxatives) is just as dangerous, for the client can lose minerals necessary for life.

Consultation

Depending on the counselor's training, skills, agency policy, and preferences, there is a usual range of clients. Sometimes a client may exceed the counselor's abilities, knowledge, or comfort level. Referral or consultation is then a good idea, and in the client's best interests. When should this be done? In addition to the examples given, when a client produces an unusual level of discomfort in me, I take this as a sign that something is amiss. If a client is beginning to express ideas of suicide, murder, or child abuse, current state laws and/or legal decisions restrict the usual cloak of confidentiality if there is reason to think that the client may be a *danger* to self or others. This does not apply to thoughts or impulses but only to behavior, or where there is some reason to think that these thoughts may be enacted soon. In such cases, securing quick consultation with a supervisor or another experienced professional is indicated. Of course when a client brings up religious themes that the counselor is persistently unclear about, then consulting with knowledgeable clergy is proper. Another, less obvious motive for consultation is when the counseling process seems to be making no forward movement even with a reasonable time and effort to get it unstuck.

Referring a Client

Referral to another professional to continue services is a more drastic step. The counselor may be having negative (and sometimes positive) emotional reactions to the client that may imperil the counseling. If consultation does not help resolve the problem, then sending the client to work with someone else is a step to consider. If the counseling process seems to be making no forward movement even with consultation, then again a referral to another counselor has to be considered. I worked with a woman who began in considerable marital and personal distress. After a good deal of progress, we settled into a comfortable routine, so I raised the topic of the lack of progress. Work began anew for a short time and then settled down again. I again raised the lack of progress and another short spurt ensued. At this point I realized the need to terminate our work and began to do this, referring my client to another professional who helped her make the progress she needed.

Sometimes a client may be working on a set of problems and much more serious difficulties emerge. The client may begin to have delusions or hallucinations or other signs of very severe problems. Discussion with someone who specializes in such areas is a first step, but again referral may be needed.

How should this be done? Some agencies have available (or require) supervision and this sort of consultation would ordinarily begin with the counselor's supervisor, but may continue to other specialists. Where referring the client elsewhere is to be considered, then this is a more serious step and if the counselor's supervisor or consultant agrees, then careful preparation of the client is important. Inevitably the client is going to feel rejected at first, even if the client knows that there is a problem. Dealing with these first feelings is very important, though trying to persuade the client that you are only acting in the client's best interests will sound like the rationalizations that parents or authority figures in the past have used. Eventually the client will likely realize this, but the initial feelings have to be dealt with.

6

Approaches to the Bible in Counseling

Most books, like the one you are now holding, have just one name. Not so the Bible. Even the usual name, Bible, from the Greek *biblios* or "books"[1] tells us that for Christianity this was *the* Book in spite of its diverse, complex, and sometimes contradictory nature. For Christians it is divided into two or three parts; the Old Testament (or Covenant), the New Testament, and, for Protestants the Apocrypha too. The Apocrypha are accepted by Catholics but regarded as doubtful for most Protestant denominations. Other names include the Holy Bible, Holy Scriptures, the Good Book, and the Word of God.

For Jews there is no Old and New Testament. They hold that their covenant with God never ended, and the Bible for Jews is largely what Christians call the Old Testament (without the Apocrypha); but the order is quite different, except for the first five books. Jews divide the Bible into three sections; *T*orah (Law or Path), *N*eviim (or Prophets) and *K*etuvim (or Writings, such as Psalms, Proverbs, Ruth and Job). The three initials *T N K* form the acronym *tanakh*, a common way Jews refer to the Bible. For Muslims, Muhammad is the "seal [end] of the prophets" and the Qur'an (or Recitation), about four-fifths as long as the New Testament, is divided into 114 chapters or *surahs*, arranged in order of decreasing length.[2]

While some Westerners find the Qur'an difficult and

tedious,[3] it is regarded most highly for its elegant and powerful poetry in the original Arabic.[4] This quality is taken as proof of its divine origin, coming from a man who was illiterate. The Qur'an declares it is without doubt or error. With a Muslim client the counselor may have to learn about the Qur'an, the *Sunna*[5] and the *Shari'a* or code of practices,[6] as well as more current standards.

Some Different Views of the Bible

The large majority of clients who present religious themes in counseling will do so from one of the many divisions within Christianity and Judaism. Often, religious instruction, family prayer, religious schooling, and church-related activities are all wrapped together and summarized as "the Bible." Not infrequently, clients who have a significant set of religious themes in their lives will know less about the Bible, either in content or origins, than one would expect from their background. Particularly when clients come from a conservative Christian background, the Bible usually means the Authorized Version, or as it is more commonly known, the King James Version. There is some trend toward use of more up-to-date versions but the sonorous, majestic language of the King James Version holds impressive sway. Such language can hide from the reader the humorous word-play and pungent, terse, earthy, and sarcastic qualities of the original Hebrew.

Humorous word-play? The Bible funny? Since when? Let me give a few examples. Adam was the first man and in Hebrew his name was *Adom*. He was created from the dust or ground, which in Hebrew is *adomah*. His name could be translated as "Dusty" or "Earthy" but not "Rocky." When the Israelites left Egypt and were wandering in the wilderness, they lived on "manna," as most people raised on Bible stories know. Apparently manna was a sweet material given off by insects in the region. When the Israelites found it on the ground, they went to Moses and said *man hu*? (Exodus 15:15) or literally "what's this?" Manna seems to be the biblical equivalent of "whatzit" or "whatchamacallit."

Pungent, terse, earthy, and sarcastic? Again, while in the wilderness (Numbers 11), the people are whining that they have had nothing to eat but this "whatzit" and they want the sort of food they had in Egypt. God tells Moses that the people will have meat for a month until it comes out from their noses and is loathsome. I think this means they will eat until they puke. Pungent and earthy! Moses says where will all this meat be found and God replies "Is the Lord's hand short?" Terse and sarcastic! No long lecture on God's power, but an answer right to the point.

The reverential tone of the King James Version obscures the respectful but direct tone of human-God conversation. The distant style of address of Thou and Thee in the King James Version is absent from the Hebrew. When God tells Abraham he is planning to destroy Sodom and Gomorrah, Abraham holds God to His own standards of justice. Moses, Jonah, Job and many others speak forthrightly to their God and get direct, if not always satisfactory answers. Such "uppitiness" was not punished. Jesus addressed God as "abba" while on the cross; this is much closer to "daddy" than "Father." The point is that many of the attitudes as well as specific ideas people think are found in the Bible do not stand up to a knowledgeable reading of the text.

Nevertheless, if you give yourself a chance to read the Bible afresh, it is like reading no other book. So much is implied without being made explicit and so little is really explained (more so in the Old Testament), yet the characters that parade across its pages are vividly realized in action and dialogue. In spite of the Bible's dramatic qualities it is only in the last century that playwrights could let dialogue and action carry their intent without use of choruses or servants to explain what was going on. For the reader open to the experience, the presence and action of God is told in human terms, but not bound by human limitations. The stories are unlike those of other peoples whose deities seem far too human and too little divine.

Translations of the Bible

To define the Bible as God's Word creates many problems. Who wrote down these words, who decided what was, or was not to be included? The Bible was recorded and transmitted by humans who did a remarkably good job of passing it down from ancient times, often telling a story that was politically unpopular, if not hazardous to their health. They tried to tell of God's presence in history[7] even if they did not intend to write objective history in its modern meaning.

As a living language Hebrew had gone out of everyday use well before the time of Jesus, and was replaced by Aramaic (a close relative of Hebrew), Greek, and other languages. So that Jews could still read the Bible, translations were made, and one of the most important, early ones was the Septuagint,[8] which brought the Hebrew Bible into Greek. It contained books that were in circulation, but were eventually not accepted by Jews when they finally closed their version of the Bible. These were incorporated into the New Testament and referred to as Apocrypha (from Greek for "hidden") by St. Jerome.

While the New Testament was written down in Greek,[9] it was by speakers of Aramaic, as some of the phrases are thought to make as good or better sense in Aramaic. To meet the needs of Latin speakers the Bible was translated again, this time into St. Jerome's authoritative Latin Vulgate (from "common people").

Thus there is some imprecision in our understanding of the text of the Bible for several reasons, including:

1. not all of the early manuscripts agree in all details,
2. sometimes the text of particular sections has been damaged,
3. some words are rare and their meaning is uncertain,
4. we do not necessarily know just what is being referred to in some parts of the text that are set in a background we may no longer understand.

This imprecision is added to by the problems of translation. When a word is used in one language, it is difficult to find exactly the same word in another. When cultures are quite different, the problem of translation is increased, and with poetry it is even worse—and the Bible contains some very powerful poetry.

An example may help. In 1 Kings 19:12, Elijah hears God's "still small voice," a phrase from the King James Version that has become fixed in our language. Other versions give a "low murmuring sound" or "sound of a gentle breeze," but the literal Hebrew is the "voice of thin silence." Josipovici[10] asks whether "still small voice" yet "works," but points out that we cannot now know how this sounded to the original hearers. And yet, I wonder if the "voice of thin silence" does not better capture Elijah's experience of hearing God's voice than all the "improvements" of the translators?

Literary Styles

In addition to the four reasons just given for problems in understanding the Bible, languages are structured differently too, and have their own literary conventions or styles. For example, "and" is a separate word in English but a prefix in Hebrew. In English, sentences rarely begin with "and" (although I just did it two sentences ago), but in biblical Hebrew it was common, and it might mean "and," "but," "however," "now," or nothing at all.[11] Another example is numbers. The number 40 frequently appears and seems to have meant a generation, or a significant period of time. One married at "40," had children at "80," and had grandchildren at "120." Thus when Moses died at 120, this meant he had grandchildren. Age was admired and esteemed in the Middle East, so the fabulously long lives of very ancient personages was a way to honor one's ancestors. Early writers tended to attach the names of great figures from the past to their work. Thus the Book of Isaiah seems to have been compiled from the work of at least three writers. The modern attitude to authorship did not exist, so the recent book *Who Wrote the Bible?*[12] misses the point. Even though the Bible contains contradictions, repetitions, and the same story told more than once with different elements, the *effect* and the *experience* is of a unified whole.

Since oral transmission of stories was a very important medium of entertainment, communication, and instruction, the story was important for many purposes.[13] The peculiar repetitions you find in reading the Bible arise from the nature of oral recitation. The stories of Jonah, Job, and Ruth, like the parables of Jesus were meant to convey a message, argue a point or struggle with a philosophical problem. They were not meant to be taken literally. For example, Jonah is sent to Nineveh "that great city," home of the brutal Assyrian kingdom hated by Jews and many other peoples, to proclaim a warning; yet the city described never existed. The message seems to be that God's salvation is available to all who repent, even the hated enemies of Israel. As mentioned earlier, Job seems to be a thoughtful struggle with the problem of evil. Ruth, written after the Jews returned from the Babylonian exile under Ezra's leadership seems to have been part of a political argument.[14]

Another important quality to keep in mind in reading

the Bible is that much is conveyed through type-scenes,[15] such as the repetitive use of meetings at the well. How these play out are related to how that particular story develops. A third aspect is the use of silence and indirection. For example, biblical Hebrew had no direct words for the genitalia or sexuality. People are introduced, or some distinctive aspect about them stated and just left. For example, early in Genesis (11–12) Sarai (Sarah, after her name was changed) is introduced as Abram's (Abraham after his name was changed) wife, and she was barren. That's all. Yet this is the crucial pivot on which the entire narrative turns. A fourth facet of biblical narrative has to do with the development of character in the narratives. Robert Alter[16] has pointed out how in Homer's *Odyssey*, Ulysses is characterized as "wily Ulysses." Such labels do not happen in the Bible because character is not fixed; rather it is the "center of surprise."[17]

Idioms and Parables

Although the Qur'an is presented as being without doubt, the issue of belief does not really arise in the Old Testament and hardly so in the New Testament. When in Acts 16:31 (in the King James Version) one reads the declaration "believe on the Lord Jesus Christ, and thou shalt be saved" it is easy to take this in its modern meaning. Belief here seems more like trust, and modern meanings of words must be used cautiously. Study and interpretation are implied in several places (Deuteronomy 6:6–7, 30:11–14; Nehemiah 8:7–8) while, as I mentioned before, several of the books are not meant to be taken at their surface meaning,[18] nor are the Parables of Jesus. More on this in a moment but it is important to deal with idioms in the Bible.

Hebrew, Aramaic, and Greek all have idioms, expressions, and metaphors and some have made their way into the English language, such as "the apple of his eye" and "set his teeth on edge." In modern English, reading that "a baseball player died at second" or "came to life in the seventh" would not make us think of Lazarus but only that his team did not hit so he could score from second base, or that he began to hit the ball better in the seventh inning. But when we read that it is easier for a camel to go through the eye of a needle than for a rich man to get into heaven (Matthew 19:23–24), it sounds like an idiom for it being impossible for the rich to go to heaven. It is an idiom, but also a *mistranslation*! The word for "camel" in Aramaic is very similar to "rope." When you read that it is easier for a rope to go through the eye of a needle than for a rich man to get into heaven, this does not mean it is impossible but that some changes will have to be made, such as removing some of the strands of the rope (that is, the materialism of the rich man).[19]

Jesus—Parables and Miracles

To many modern readers the New Testament Gospels seem filled with charming, powerful stories (parables) and miraculous happenings which either persuade or leave the reader doubtful and incredulous. Let us consider the parables first. Such stories undoubtedly had a long tradition since Jesus lived in an oral society, and he uses them for effective instruction.[20] The Old Testament is replete with orally transmitted narratives and the Talmud also contained many such parables, sometimes with "miraculous" events as part of the story, which were designed to make a point and give the story color.

The parables, apparently simple stories, are actually quite compact and need thought and elaboration to become unfolded. A good example discussed by Josipovici[21] is that of the prodigal son, which is sometimes interpreted as contrasting the elder son (Israel) and the younger son (Christianity). But if you do not know what is supposed to be there, this is a story of a father's love and the corrosive effects of jealousy. A step beyond is to see the repetitive theme of favoritism by fathers (and sometimes mothers) toward younger (or special) sons. Finally the father's lack of fairness either leads the reader to recoil and reject the story or to stretch beyond the story and hear perhaps "the voice of thin silence."

I was once approached by a young missionary woman who engaged me in a discussion about religion and she asked how I explained the miracles in the New Testament, and especially the Resurrection. What she eventually got to was that because of these miracles I should believe as she did and convert to Christianity. My explanation that Jesus lived on after His crucifixion in the hearts and experience of his followers[22] was not persuasive and we agreed to see things differently. To some readers the various miracles seem a disruption to the narrative, as we have a different view of the world. If a person returns to life today, we expect to see all of modern technology. It is only when the stories in the four Gospels of the New Testament are compared with discoveries of Nag Hammadi and other apocryphal fragments that we can see how *few* miracles are in Matthew, Mark, Luke, and John and how these miracles make a point or serve someone's needs. In the gospels excluded from the Bible, Jesus is described as performing many more miracles, which often serve no purpose other than to prove his power, and even portray Jesus as mean, cruel, or petty. As elsewhere, the Bible speaks on many levels. Reading it is only the first step.

Modern Translations

With the exception of the *Anchor Bible* series, which is translated by internationally recognized scholars whose emphasis is objectivity, most translations are sponsored by one or more denominations, and these have particular points of view. So, even if the same Hebrew or Greek text is being used, somewhat different renditions are likely to occur. If a specific text is important to a client then it may be useful to compare parallel translations of that part of the Bible.[23]

The client's denominational affiliation may also limit the range of choices of translations. Conservative Protestant denominations are likely to favor the *Authorized Version* (King James), the *New King James Version* and the *New American Standard Bible*. Some evangelical (i.e., outreach, activist) churches may employ the *Bible in Basic English*, the *Good News Bible*, the *Living Bible Paraphrased*, or similar materials which offer translations without a strict adherence to the text, and freely delete portions not central to the story. Mainline Protestant denominations are likely to rely on the *Revised Standard Version*, the *New English Bible*, the *Interpreter's Bible* and sometimes the *Jerusalem Bible*. Both the *Jerusalem Bible*, which is a carefully done French version translated into English, and the *New American Bible* were produced under Catholic auspices. The *Soncino Books of the Bible* (in fourteen volumes) has a King James-style English translation with parallel Hebrew text, and this and *The Holy Scriptures* have been two standard bibles relied upon for general use in Jewish congregations. Recently, the Jewish Publication Society has issued a new translation of *The Holy Scriptures* in modern English that seems likely to replace older ones.

Many of these editions come with introductory or explanatory material that will describe historical background and reveal alternative meanings which can aid the reader's understanding. *The Anchor Bible*, *Interpreter's Bible* and the *Soncino Books of the Bible* all contain very extensive background materials. Some editions of the *Jerusalem Bible* contain useful information, but not as detailed as the previous three. Many of these translations contain headings or captions that give the reader guides as to content and the direction the text is going. Initially helpful, these headings also steer the reader in ways different from what might occur if the reader was having a more direct experience in reading the text.[24]

But Is It Really True?

Most professionally trained counselors and social workers receive their training in secular institutions (public or private universities) and these value their intellectual independence in their quest for the truth. The student with a religious affiliation often learns to keep that part of his or her life private, and many students have little more than conventional religious connections that are confined to formal observance of major holidays. If a student has taken courses in the humanities, English, or the academic study of religion, he or she will have probably encountered studies of the Bible (often called "higher criticism") that will develop the idea that the core of the Old Testament (the first 5 books; *Torah* or Pentateuch) is collected from several components, sources or strands. Typically, four such components are identified: *J* (where God is named as Jehovah), *E* (where God is referred to as Elohim), *P* (portions thought to have been written by the Priestly party) and *D* (attributed to the writer of Deuteronomy). The simple story told to children about God's authorship of the Bible no longer serves college-educated professionals very well and they have little to fall back on. Adult religion deals with difficult, and sometimes very abstract ideas, and the college student is unprepared. Much personal religious belief goes by the board, leaving behind the bitter sense of having been fooled by trusted adult authorities.

While the simple story about the Bible's origins may no longer serve the adult, these biblical scholars have not had the last word either. In spite of the different languages, literary styles, silences, and ambiguities, a coherence and unity exists that people have sensed for a long time, even when they could not have explained it well. Some of this unity has been developed in several recent studies of the Bible using methods of literary criticism.[25]

The question that heads this section is the sort of question our modern age asks. By "true" we usually mean, did it happen? can you prove it? is there evidence? and so on. This question is not answerable in this way for many reasons, including that it covers too much. But for clients for whom the Bible may be important, the question can be rewritten as *But Is It Really Valid*? That is, can these people find meanings, guidance, and relationships through their understanding of the Bible that enhances their lives? This is a question that each person must answer individually.

Notes

Introduction

1. Only Malta, Ireland, and Mexico report higher frequencies of church attendance while eighteen countries report lower rates, including Spain (41 percent), Italy (36 percent), France (12 percent) and Iceland, with the lowest rate at 3 percent. C. H. Jacquet, Jr., *Yearbook of American & Canadian Churches 1987*. (Nashville: Abingdon Press, 1987).

2. The national weekly church and synagogue attendance is 42 percent, with men somewhat less frequent (36 percent) than women (49 percent). Similarly, attendance steadily increases with age, rising from a low of 31 percent for persons 18–24 year old to 49 percent for those 65 and older. Jacquet, *Yearbook of American & Canadian Churches 1987*.

Chapter 1: The Helping Professions and Religion

1. A simple example is in 1 Samuel 1:12–17 in which Hannah, who is childless, prays silently for a child. The priest Eli assumes she is drunk and urges her to give up her drinking. She explains what she is doing and Eli replies with encouragement.

2. P. L. Entralgo, *The Therapy of the Word in Classical Antiquity*, trans. L. J. Rather and J. M. Sharp (New Haven: Yale University Press, 1970).

3. Wisdom, is distinct from intelligence (which has a long research history in modern psychology) and is only just beginning to be studied scientifically. P. Baltes is currently reporting on experimental studies of wisdom.

4. R. B. Y. Scott, *Proverbs & Ecclesiastes*, in *The Anchor Bible* (Garden City, NY: Doubleday & Co., 1983), Proverbs 10:4.

5. Scott, *Anchor Bible*, Proverbs 13:24. Note the repetitive

statements on this theme in Proverbs (10:13; 22:15; 23:13–14; 29:15). Although a study of their variations is interesting, their repetitive nature indicates that the Jews addressed by these statements were indulgent parents.

6. R. J. Lovinger, *Working with Religious Issues in Therapy* (New York: Jason Aronson, 1984). Books such as *Jonah* deal with the nature of the prophetic calling, *Job* with the problem in understanding evil, and *Ruth* is probably connected with political opposition to the reforms of Ezra after the return from the Babylonian exile.

7. J. Jaynes, *The Origins of Consciousness in the Breakdown of the Bicameral Mind* (Boston: Houghton-Miflin, 1976).

Our word for "idiot" arises from the Greek for a citizen who takes no interest in the political and civic affairs of his city.

8. E. N. Jackson, *Parish Counseling* (New York: Jason Aronson, 1975). C. A. Wise, *Pastoral Psychotherapy* (New York: Jason Aronson, 1980).

There are a number of programs that provide sophisticated training for clergy in pastoral counseling and in psychotherapy, including ones at the Menninger Foundation in Topeka, Kansas and at the Postgraduate Center for the Mental Health in New York.

9. William Meissner and William McFadden are both Jesuit priests and psychoanalysts. Meissner was president of the Boston Psychoanalytic Society. Other work settings include community mental health services and industrial counseling. *Behavior Today* (15 June, 1981).

10. C. Ragan, H. N. Malony, and B. Beit-Hallahmi, "Psychologists and Religion: Professional Factors and Personal Belief," *Review of Religious Research* (1980) 21:208–17.

J. D. Gartner, "Christians Need not Apply: Religious Discrimination in Clinical Psychology Graduate Admissions" (Paper delivered at the American Psychological Association Convention, 1982).

———, "Religious Prejudice in Psychology: Theories of its Cause and Cure" (Paper delivered at the American Psychological Association Convention, 1983).

11. Lovinger, *Religious Issues in Therapy.*

M. H. Spero, *Psychotherapy With the Religious Patient,* (Springfield, IL: C. C. Thomas, 1985).

E. M. Stern, *Psychotherapy and the Religiously Committed Patient,* (New York: The Haworth Press, 1985).

12. G. Ahlskog, "Latent Theology: A Clinical Perspective on *The Future of an Illusion,*" in *Psychotherapy and the Religiously Committed Patient,* ed. E. Mark Stern (New York: The Haworth Press, 1985), 63.

13. Described in more detail in Lovinger, *Religious Issues in Therapy.*

14. T. Robbins and D. Anthony, "'Cults' in the Late Twentieth Century," in *Encyclopedia of the American Religious Experience,* ed. C. H. Lippy and P. W. Williams (New York: Charles Scribner's Sons, 1988), 741–54.

15. P. Gay, *Freud, A Life for Our Time* (New York: Norton, 1988).

16. Oskar Pfister, *Christianity and Fear,* cited by W. E. Oates, "The Diagnostic Use of the Bible," *Pastoral Psychology* 1,9 (1950):43–46.

17. S. Freud, *The Future of an Illusion* (New York: Norton, 1927).

18. E. L. Worthington, Jr., "Religious Counseling: A Review of Published Empirical Research," *Journal of Counseling and Development* 64 (1986):421–31.

19. J. C. Hansen, R. R. Stevic and R. W. Warner, Jr., *Counseling: Theory and Process* (Boston: Allyn and Bacon, 1972).

R. L. George and T. S. Cristiani, *Theory, Methods and Processes of Counseling and Psychotherapy* (Englewood Cliffs, NJ: Prentice-Hall, 1981).

20. P. Rieff, *Freud: The Mind of the Moralist* (New York: Viking, 1959).

21. As cited in ed. C. H. Lippy and P. W. Williams, *Encyclopedia of the American Religious Experience* (New York: Charles Scribner's Sons, 1988), vii.

22. The number of Christians in the world has increased by over 250 percent in this century, although the proportion of Christians has remained stable, declining slightly from 34.4 percent in 1900 to 32.8 percent in 1980. Islam has grown by over 360 percent, which represents an increase from 12.4 per-

cent to 16.5 percent in the same eighty-year period. *Time,* (May 3, 1982), 66.

23. M. Argyle and B. Beit-Hallahmi, *The Social Psychology of Religion,* (London: Routledge & Kegan Paul, 1975), 1.

24. P. L. Berger, "Some Second Thoughts on Substantive Versus Functional Definitions of Religion," *Journal for the Scientific Study of Religion* 13 (1974):125–33.

25. Suggested by Joseph Frankenfield.

26. J. Wilson, *Encyclopedia of the American Religious Experience.* ed. Lippy and Williams, 17.

27. Maimonides, whose correct name is Moses ben Maimon and is also known as the *Rambam* (an acronym for *Ra*bbi *M*oses *b*en *M*aimon), was a physician who became the preeminent medieval Jewish scholar. Credited with many scholarly accomplishments, he made the science of his day compatible with Jewish thought.

28. Pharisee is derived from the Hebrew *perush* meaning separate. The Pharisees were a group who were active in presenting a form of Jewish life in which the common people could participate, as distinct from the Temple worship controlled by the priests or Sadducees (descendants of the priestly family of *Zadok*). Jesus's quarrel with the Pharisees is frequently misunderstood as a rejection of their views rather than an objection to some individuals who were deficient in observance or devotion.

29. Jews date their history from the creation of the world, presumably 5750 years ago and roughly equivalent to 1990; Christians from the accepted date of the birth of Jesus, and Muslims from Muhammad's flight from Mecca to Medina 622 years later. The Christian calendar dating is now near universal, but in partial recognition of other traditions, I will use C.E. (for Common Era) and B.C.E. (for Before the Common Era).

30. Another list of the main points might be the Incarnation, the Atonement and the Trinity. See H. Smith, *The Religions of Man* (New York: Harper & Row, 1958).

31. Not all denominations would agree; for some the world was good but is now evil, and for others it is evil and needing redemption or destruction.

32. *Qur'an* is the more correct transliteration of Koran, just

as *Muhammad* is more exact than Mohammed, and *Muslim* is more precise than Moslem.

33. N. S. Booth, Jr., "Islam in North America," *Encyclopedia of the American Religious Experience,* ed. Lippy and Williams, 723–29.

34. *Time,* (Feb. 11, 1988), 49–50.

35. Lovinger, *Religious Issues in Therapy.*

36. *Time,* (May 3, 1982), 66.

37. A. J. Raboteau, "Black Christianity in North America," *Encyclopedia of the American Religious Experience,* ed. Lippy and Williams, 638.

38. "Black Churches: Can They Strengthen the Black Family?" *Carnegie Quarterly* 33 (1987–88):1–7.

39. J. Shipps, "The Latter-Day Saints," *Encyclopedia of the American Religious Experience,* ed. Lippy and Williams, 649–65.

40. C. H. Lippy, "Millenialism and Adventism," *Encyclopedia of the American Religious Experience,* ed. Lippy and Williams, 831–44.

41. Lovinger, *Religious Issues in Therapy.*

Chapter 2: American Religions and Their Implications for Counseling

1. Paraphrased from a remark by Sidney Smith of the Menninger Foundation.

2. T. Szasz, *The Ethics of Psychoanalysis* (New York: Dell, 1965).

3. The *Tarasoff* decisions and other case law relating to therapist responsibility for client dangerousness to others are particularly noteworthy. Most, if not all states have mandatory child abuse reporting laws, while abuse of the elderly is becoming a matter of increasing public concern. Failure to act when there is plausible suicidal risk comes under the "standard of care" doctrine in case and statute law. These are matters that are continuing to change on a rapid basis.

4. H. Watson and M. Levine, "Psychotherapy and Mandated Reporting of Child Abuse," *American Journal of Orthopsychiatry* 59 (1989):246–56. Although they reported that when therapists disclosed child abuse to Protective Services agencies there were

sometimes improvements in the treatment working relationship, negative results were equally likely. No change seemed the most probable outcome.

5. See J. E. Adams, *Competent to Counsel* (Nutley, NJ: Presbyterian and Reformed Publishing Co., 1970).

J. M. Vayhinger, "Protestantism (Conservative-Evangelical) and the Therapist, in *Religious Systems and Psychotherapy,* ed. R. H. Cox (Springfield, IL: C. C. Thomas, 1973), 56–71.

A. E. Bergin, "Psychotherapy and Religious Values," *Journal of Consulting and Clinical Psychology* 48 (1980):95–105.

———, "Religious and Humanistic Values: A Reply to Ellis and Walls," *Journal of Consulting and Clinical Psychology* 48 (1980):642–45.

A. Ellis, "Psychotherapy and Atheistic Values: A Response to A. E. Bergin's 'Psychotherapy and Religious Values,'" *Journal of Consulting and Clinical Psychology* 48 (1980):635–39.

G. B. Walls, "Values and Psychotherapy: A Comment on 'Psychotherapy and Religious Values,'" *Journal of Consulting and Clinical Psychology* 48 (1980):640–41.

6. R. J. Lovinger, *Working With Religious Issues in Therapy* (New York: Jason Aronson, 1984).

P. Rieff, *Freud: The Mind of the Moralist* (New York: Viking, 1959).

7. S. A. Appelbaum, "The Dangerous Edge of Insight," *Psychotherapy: Theory, Research and Practice* 13 (1976):202–6.

8. P. Wachtel, "What Should We Say to our Patients?: On the Wording of Therapists' Comments," *Psychotherapy: Theory, Research and Practice* 17 (1980):183–88.

9. There is an expanding literature on this topic. See D. M. Berger, *Clinical Empathy* (Northvale, NJ: Jason Aronson, 1987).

10. A very good example is given in the Introduction of P. L. Wachtel, *Psychoanalysis and Behavior Therapy: Toward an Integration* (New York: Basic Books, 1977). Here a skilled behavior therapist was observed by Wachtel working with a resistant patient who indirectly sabotaged his own stated goal of improving his heterosexual social skills.

11. H. S. Kaplan, *The New Sex Therapy* (New York: Brunner/Mazel, 1974).

12. An illuminating and persuasive case is made by Gardner

for the existence of two types of personal intelligences (interpersonal and intrapersonal). Both appear necessary for effective counseling. He suggests that personal counseling or psychotherapy works to enhance these skills.

H. Gardner *Frames of Mind: The Theory of Multiple Intelligences* (New York: Basic Books, 1983).

13. I prefer *religiousness* to *religiosity,* which has unwarranted implications of pathology.

14. From a paper, "Severely Disturbed Patients and Religious Ideation," read at the Genesee County Community Mental Health Center, Flint, MI, May 1988.

15. This is discussed somewhat more fully in relation to religion in Lovinger, *Religious Issues in Therapy* and is based on the work of F. R. Kluckhohn and F. L. Strodtbeck, *Variations in Value Orientations* (New York: Row, Peterson, 1961).

16. This is well expressed in a verse by Ogden Nash:

How odd of God,
To choose the Jews.

See also: M. Dimont, *Jews, God and History* (New York: Simon and Schuster, 1962).

17. R. B. Y. Scott, *Proverbs & Ecclesiastes, The Anchor Bible,* 2nd ed. (Garden City, NY: Doubleday & Co., 1983), 186.

18. The Talmud, a codification of Jewish law and lore, story and science, which originated several centuries before the Common Era, contains rabbinic debates in which both the majority and minority opinion are recorded. Sometimes the minority opinion eventually prevailed, and sometimes the sages were overruled by the populace. In one classic story, the rabbis are debating a point where all are disagreeing with one of the group. The dissident produces three miracles to convince his colleagues, who reject this. Finally heaven is invoked, but the rabbis tell God not to intervene. The story closes with God gleefully telling one of the prophets that his children have defeated him.

19. The word for prayer in Hebrew is derived from a word meaning to pray, judge or examine. In the conjugation used, prayer could mean self-examination.

20. M. J. Weaver, "The Roman Catholic Heritage," in *Encyclopedia of the American Religious Experience* ed. C. H. Lippy and

P. W. Williams, (New York: Charles Scribner's Sons, 1988), 153–70.

21. P. D. Garrett, "Eastern Christianity," in *Encyclopedia of the American Religious Experience* ed. Lippy and Williams, 325–44.

22. Weaver, "The Roman Catholic Heritage," *Encyclopedia of the American Religious Experience* ed. Lippy and Williams.

23. C. H. Jacquet, Jr., *Yearbook of American & Canadian Churches 1987* (Nashville: Abingdon Press, 1987).

24. Mortal sins are those (1) that are more serious acts, (2) that the person knows are wrong, and (3) have the full consent of the will. Venial sins are (1) less serious and (2) consent of the will is less certain. In Catholic thought one cannot sin by accident, while in the Old Testament most sin was referred to by the Hebrew *chet* (pronounced with a strongly aspirated "h"). This word is derived from archery and means to miss the mark, i.e., to make an error. Accidental error (sin) was thus likely.

25. D. B. Barrett, *World Christian Encyclopedia: A Comparative Study of Churches and Religions in the Modern World, A.D. 1900–2000* (Oxford: Oxford University Press, 1982).

26. List adapted from Lovinger, *Religious Issues in Therapy* and derived from one that was proposed earlier by F. E. Mayer, *The Religious Bodies of America,* 4th ed. (St. Louis: Concordia Publishing House, 1961).

27. This grouping differs partially from that offered in *Working With Religious Issues in Therapy.*

28. Sacraments are variously defined, but may be understood as acts that bring about the experience of God's loving care (grace).

29. Mayer, *Religious Bodies of America.*

30. Original sin is usually understood to mean Adam and Eve's disobedience to God by eating the fruit (the Bible never said apple) of the tree of the knowledge of good and evil. A more radical interpretation may be that Adam and Eve tried to transcend their essential limitations and become like God by trying to acquire this knowledge, and thus rejected their need for God. This need to transcend may be understood as their awareness of their inability to merit God's concern. I am indebted to Joseph Frankenfield for this suggestion.

31. B. Tipson, "Calvinist Heritage," *Encyclopedia of the American Religious Experience,* ed. Lippy and Williams, 451–56.

32. For Mormons these are *The Book of Mormon, Pearl of Great Price,* and *Doctrines and Covenants.* For Christian Scientists this is *Science and Health with Key to the Scriptures.*

33. M. Barinaga, "Can Psychotherapy Delay Cancer Deaths?" *Science* 246 (1989):448–49.

34. J. L. Sheler, "Healing an Ailing Church," *U. S. News & World Report* (Nov. 6, 1989), 75–76.

35. H. Montague, "The Pessimistic Sect's Influence on the Mental Health of its Members: The Case of Jehovah's Witnesses," *Social Compass* 24 (1977): 135–47.

H. Botting & G. Botting, *The Orwellian World of Jehovah's Witnesses* (Toronto: University of Toronto Press, 1984).

36. From Greek, meaning "God in them," or inspired.

37. Why this particular issue has become so important is far from clear. I suspect that many fundamentalists feel a general loss of control in their lives, control which has shifted to the technically-oriented members of society. Insistence on Creationism represents an attack on a generally accepted scientific principle that is still accessible, sufficiently non-technical and has enough unknowns to be confronted with Bible excerpts. Ironically, the description of the sequence of Creation in Genesis is remarkably close to established scientific views. Most creation myths are absurd; Genesis is not. Even a greater irony is that many scientists of the nineteenth century, including Darwin, were believers. Religious belief is probably lower among physical scientists than among Americans in general, but it is higher than among social scientists.

38. A similar-seeming event is described in Acts 2:1–13, which occurred at the time of Pentecost. However in Acts 2, what is described is people conversing in other languages, while in Acts 19, it would appear that it was similar to glossolalia, where a person vocalizes but it is not a language. Pentecost (derived from "fifty" in Greek) refers to the early harvest festival of *Shavuot* (from "fifty" in Hebrew) which occurs fifty days after Passover.

39. D. G. Bromley and A. D. Shupe, Jr., *Strange Gods: The Great American Cult Scare* (Boston: Beacon Press, 1981).

40. D. B. Barrett, *World Christian Encyclopedia.*

41. L. H. Mamiya and C. E. Lincoln, "Black Militant and Separatist Movements," in *Encyclopedia of the American Religious Experience* ed. Lippy and Williams, 755–71.

Chapter 3: Religious Themes in the Life of the Person

1. Albert Ellis epitomizes the view of religion as essentially pathological, although he expresses a modest tolerance for its more liberal forms of expression. Freud's concepts were much more sophisticated and complex, dealing with both pathology and various cultural issues and speculations.

2. The work of Jay Adams in *Competent to Counsel* and related publications exemplifies this approach.

3. P. W. Pruyser, *A Dynamic Psychology of Religion* (New York: Harper & Row, 1968).

4. Pruyser, *Dynamic Psychology of Religion,* 73.

5. David Elkind has studied developmental changes in the child's conception of religious identity, using a Piaget-style interview, and has found that young children evinced at least three definable stages. In the first stage (5–7), children often confused religious and ethnic or other designations; in the second stage (7–9), religious identity was equated with specific behaviors; while in the third stage (10–12), a more abstract conception of religious identity, tied to belief or faith, emerged. Jewish and Catholic children had a clearer sense of identity in the first stage than Protestant children. In the second stage Jewish children perceived differences based on home and family activity, while Christian children identified distinctions based on church activities. D. Elkind, "Age Changes in the Meaning of Religious Identity," *Review of Religious Research* 6 (1964):36–40.

———, "The Origins of Religion in the Child," *Review of Religious Research* 12 (1970):35–42.

6. Piaget identifies this age as the one most likely to see the beginnings of Formal Operational (i.e., abstract) thought.

7. Belief comes from Old English, and one of its meaning is "by love." In older translations of the Bible, "belief" was the translation for words that better meant trust, confidence, steadiness, reliance. Only rarely did belief refer to persuasion, or to thought or ideas.

8. "Miracle" is often the modern word but this is from the

fourth century Latin Vulgate. The Old Testament refers to "signs" or "wonders," while the New Testament refers to "signs" or "acts of power."

9. See Hans Küng for a committed, sophisticated but nonderogatory view of such "propaganda" in *On Being a Christian* (Garden City, NY: Doubleday & Co., 1976).

10. An orange and a banana are both fruit, which is a common, full-credit abstraction on the Similarities Subtest of the Wechsler Adult Intelligence Test. One could also say they are both grown from trees, both of the vegetable kingdom, both natural features of the earth, both aspects of the universe, and both created by God. "Both grown from trees" only secures half-credit while the rest of these abstractions are scored zero and are more frequently seen in psychotic records.

11. Pruyser, *Dynamic Psychology of Religion.*

12. Albert Ellis's Rational-Emotive therapy is similarly based, going beyond scientific methodology and conceptions to a form of scientism as a basis for ordering one's life.

13. One example of this is the overall thrust in Judaism toward life and its legitimate enjoyment. See Leviticus 26:3–5; Deuteronomy 8:7–10; 30:19–20. The Hebrews were strongly enjoined to observe the Sabbath and do no work. If a city or a person is attacked on the Sabbath, self-defense entails work. This clash of principles involves a boundary condition. One choice is to permit the attack on the principle that God will provide, or this is punishment for sin. A second is to disregard the Sabbath. A third is to decide that one can violate the Sabbath to preserve life. Ancient Hebrew scholars decided that all commandments could be broken to preserve life except committing murder, idolatry or gross immorality.

14. Pruyser, *Dynamic Psychology of Religion,* 95. This is exemplified in note 10., in which an orange and banana are grouped as both being part of the universe, or created by God.

15. For Jews the *Old* Testament is not "old." See chapter 6 for more detail.

16. These primarily pivot around the divinity of Jesus. Not a small problem to Christianity, the difficulties for Judaism may be simply expressed in the statement, "Anything that can be created is not God." (I am indebted to R. Jossef Kratzenstein for this concise statement.)

17. The Book of Revelation is probably the most extreme

of this sort, although remarkable imagery is found elsewhere, as in Ezekiel.

18. This includes Proverbs, Psalms, Ecclesiastes (or Kohelet), Job, the Wisdom of Solomon, and Ecclesiasticus (or Ben Sirach). The latter two are in the Apocrypha (from the Greek for "hidden").

19. Pruyser, *Dynamic Psychology of Religion.* This list is based on the famous work *On Religion* published by Schleiermacher in 1799.

20. P. W. Pruyser, "Forms and Functions of the Imagination in Religion," *Bulletin of the Menninger Clinic* 49 (1985):353–70.

21. *Kavanah* is difficult to translate but concentration or devotion are approximate. The term especially refers to an attitude in prayer. In addition to compassion or mercy, there is an emphasis on charity or *tzedekah* (the word also means justice).

22. Extended examples are given in chapter 6. One such literal translation is J. Magil, *Magil's Linear School Bible* (New York: Hebrew Publishing Co., 1905).

23. This is epitomized in Edward Gibbon's epigram, first published in 1776, which stated that, in Rome, all religions "were considered by the people as equally true; by the philosopher as equally false; and by the magistrate as equally useful." *The Decline and Fall of the Roman Empire* vol. 1, (New York: The Heritage Press, 1946), 22. Compare Karl Marx's aphorism of religion as the opiate of the people.

24. P. W. Pruyser, *Between Belief and Unbelief* (New York: Harper & Row, 1974).

25. M. Douglas, *Purity and Danger: An Analysis of Concepts of Pollution and Taboo* (New York: Praeger, 1966).

26. Much of this section is based on the following: R. J. Lovinger, "The Religious Patient—Theory and Some Treatment Issues." (Paper delivered at the Third International meeting of the Association for Mental Health Affiliation with Israel. Jerusalem, Israel, 1986).

27. The sensory deprivation studies and studies of the effects of stimulation on brain weight in rats clearly indicate the importance of sensory input to brain function.

28. One type of meaning-system is a theory which helps organize data.

29. S. B. Pomeroy, *Goddesses, Whores, Wives and Slaves: Women*

in Classical Antiquity (New York: Schocken Books, 1975). She reviews several methods, both effective and ineffective, employed for abortion and contraception in the ancient world.

30. J. Leo, "The Moral Complexity of Choice," *U.S. News & World Report* (Dec. 4, 1989), 64.

31. R. J. Lovinger, *Religious Issues in Therapy* (New York: Jason Aronson, 1984). This topic was also discussed in chapter 1 in the section comparing counseling, psychotherapy, and ministry.

32. J. Leo, "The Moral Complexity of Choice."

33. C. Holden, "Koop Finds Abortion Evidence 'Inconclusive,'" *Science* 243 (1989):730–31.

34. C. Holden, "Koop Finds Abortion Evidence 'Inconclusive.'"

35. M. Abdul-Rauf, *The Islamic View of Women and the Family* (New York: Robert Speller & Sons, 1977).

36. C. Holden, "Is Alcoholism a Disease?" *Science* 238 (1987):1647.

37. D. L. Ohlms, *The Disease Concept of Alcoholism* (Belleville, IL: Gary Whiteaker Co., 1983).

38. Estimates are that about 70 percent of adults drink alcohol in some form but that only about one-eighth of this group become alcoholic.

39. H. J. Shaffer, "The Disease Controversy: Of Metaphors, Maps & Menus," *Journal of Psychoactive Drugs* 16 (1984):1–12.

This article surveys some interesting history of attitudes toward addictive "diseases" as well as thoughtful criticisms of the disease model.

40. C. Holden, "Is Alcoholism Treatment Effective?" *Science* 236 (1987):20-22.

41. Alcohol and drugs are reported to produce pleasure at first, but later in the use cycle, drugs are frequently reported as consumed to stave off depression, physical reactions, "crashing," and so on.

42. D. M. Barnes, "Breaking the Cycle of Addiction," *Science* 241 (1988):1029–30. This reports a study which indicates that a combination of medication (desipramine), behavior therapy (extinction), and psychotherapy is quite effective with cocaine addiction, whereas alone, none of these interventions had long-term effects.

C. Holden, "*Is Alcoholism Treatment Effective?*" Current data suggests that inpatient treatment is not better as a whole than outpatient or other briefer, less expensive treatments. The report also noted the marked variability in types of alcoholics and the diversity of outcomes. Inpatient treatment is becoming increasingly popular in the United States in complex for-profit programs.

43. R. D. Martin, *Islam: A Cultural Perspective* (Englewood Cliffs, NJ: Prentice-Hall, 1982).

F. M. Denny, *Islam* (San Francisco: Harper & Row, 1987).

44. This is a very long section (Job 38:1–7, 16–18, 39–41) so only a little will be quoted from *The Anchor Bible,* trans. M. H. Pope, 3rd ed. (Garden City, NY: Doubleday & Co., 1983).

38:1–7

Then Yahweh answered Job

From out of the storm and said:

"Who is this that obscures counsel
With words void of knowledge?

Gird your loins like a hero,

I will ask and you will tell me.

Where were you when I founded the earth?
Tell me, if you know so much.

Who drafted its dimensions?
Surely You know?
Who stretched the line over it?

16–18

Have you entered the springs of the sea,
Walked in the recesses of the deep?

Have Death's Gates been revealed to you,
Have you seen the Dark Portals?

Have you examined the earth's expanse?
Tell if you know all this.

39-41

Can you hunt prey for the lioness,
Appease the appetite of her cubs,

When they crouch in their den,
Lie in wait in their lair?

On what are its sockets sunk,
Who laid its cornerstone,

While the morning stars sang
together
And all the Gods exulted?

Who provides the raven prey,
When its fledglings cry to God,
Frantic for lack of food?

45. D. L. Rosenhan and M. E. P. Seligman, *Abnormal Psychology* (New York: Norton, 1984), 307.

46. M. Barinaga, "Manic Depression Gene Put in Limbo," *Science* 246 (1989):886–87.

47. P. R. Breggin, *Electroshock: Its Brain-Disabling Effects* (New York: Springer Publishing Co., 1979).

R. Abrams, "Out of the Blue," *The Sciences* 29, 6 (1989):25–30.

48. G. B. Kolata, "Clinical Trial of Psychotherapies is Under Way," *Science* 212 (1981):432–33.

J. Leo, "Talk is as Good as a Pill," *Time* (May 26, 1986).

49. S. Freud, "Mourning and Melancholia," *Collected Papers of Sigmund Freud* Vol. IV (London: Hogarth Press, 1950), 152–70. Although more than seventy years old, Freud's paper can still be read with profit both for understanding of severe depression and for methods of treatment.

50. A. T. Beck, A. J. Rush, B. F. Shaw, and G. Emery, *Cognitive Therapy of Depression* (New York: The Guilford Press, 1979). Beck's approach parallels that of Albert Ellis's rational-emotive therapy.

51. M. E. P. Seligman, *Helplessness: On Depression, Development and Death* (San Francisco: Freeman, 1975).

M. E. P. Seligman, L. Y. Abramson, A. Semmel, and C. von Baeyer, "Depressive Attributional Style," *Journal of Abnormal Psychology* 88 (1979):242–47. This approach (learned helplessness) has developed into the concept of hopelessness depression, and has been exploring depressed persons' view of the world and their expectations (attributions) about external events and their ability to affect their world.

52. A. T. Beck et al., *Cognitive Therapy of Depression.*

53. Albert Ellis holds very critical, negative views on the value

of religion in the life of clients. At least one study in his own institute suggests that religious clients are no more troubled than nonreligious clients. Ellis's views on religion do not automatically disqualify rational-emotive therapy as a treatment of religious clients.

54. Results of a Gallup poll reported in *Psychology Today* 22 (1988):8.

55. The Constitutional prohibition against cruel and unusual punishment dealt with the then current practices of torturous punishments and executions (mostly of men, although women and children were frequently mistreated too).

56. J. Kaufman and E. Zigler, "Do Abused Children Become Abusive Parents?" *American Journal of Orthopsychiatry* 57 (1987):186–92.

C. S. Widom, "Child Abuse, Neglect and Adult Behavior: Research Design and Findings on Criminality, Violence, and Child Abuse," *American Journal of Orthopsychiatry* 59 (1989): 355–67.

It is commonly thought that if they were abused as children, adults will abuse their own children. The intergenerational transmission rate is about thirty percent, serious, but far from a fixed transfer.

57. Sigmund Freud made this remark. A similar point is implied in B. F. Skinner's concept of the power of positive reinforcement to shape behavior.

58. This phrase is actually from a poem by Blake.

59. C. Watkins, *Indo-European and the Indo-Europeans,* vol. 2 of *The Heritage Illustrated Dictionary of the English Language* (Boston: Houghton-Miflin, 1979), 1496–550.

1. *Grace,* from Latin *gratia* (pleasure, favor, thanks), from Indo-European *gwere-* (to praise aloud).
2. *Heal* from Old English *hal* (hale, whole), from Indo-European *kailo-* (whole, uninjured, of good omen).
3. *Salvation* from Latin *solidus* (solid) to a Latin variant of *salvus* (whole, safe, uninjured), from Indo-European *sol-* (whole).

60. This includes evangelical, fundamentalist, pentecostal and holiness churches. A similar movement may be found among Catholics in the charismatic movement. See J. D. Hunter, *American Evangelicalism: Conservative Religion and the Quandary*

of Modernity (New Brunswick, NJ: Rutgers University Press, 1983).

61. J. Money, *Gay, Straight and In-between* (New York: Oxford University Press, 1988).

62. Many societies allow for homosexual behavior, ranging from its being considered a regular developmental stage for all males, to its being disapproved of but permitted.

63. Homosexuality was once a psychiatric diagnosis, but was dropped after vigorous protests from gay activist groups.

64. AIDS (Acquired Immune Deficiency Syndrome), ARC (Aids Related Complex) and HIV (Human Immunodeficiency Virus) are some of the current terms. AIDS and related conditions are not, of course, confined to gay men, although the disease first made an appearance in this country among that group. In Africa, AIDS is primarily a disease among heterosexuals.

65. In working with clients, it is generally preferable to use their language. "Gay" used to be a generic term among homosexuals to designate themselves but this has more recently been used to designate male homosexuals. "Lesbian" refers to female homosexuals, "bi" or bisexual refers to people who are sexually active with both genders, and "straight" refers to heterosexuals. There are a large number of slang terms but I will use the generally accepted terms of straight, gay, lesbian, and bisexual.

66. Leviticus 18:22; 20:13, Romans 1:18–32, I Corinthians 6:9–10, I Timothy 1:9–10. If the bulk of the full text of the Bible is compared to these five prohibitions of homosexuality, it is clear that the Bible's writers' attention was primarily elsewhere. For example, in the first five books (*Torah* or Mosaic law) the commandment not to annoy, harass or mistreat the stranger is repeated *thirty-six* times while homosexuality is prohibited twice!

67. Lovinger, *Religious Issues in Therapy.* This topic is dealt with in somewhat more detail here. *Human Sexuality: New Directions in American Catholic Thought,* by A. Kosnik, W. Carroll, A. Cunningham, R. Modias, and J. Schulte, (Mahwah, NJ: Paulist Press, 1977) is an excellent source. Also worthwhile are W. G. Coles, *Sex and Love in the Bible* (New York: Association Press, 1959) and R. Patai, *Family, Love and the Bible* (London: MacGibbon and Kee, 1960).

68. R. Scroggs, *The New Testament and Homosexuality* (Philadelphia: Fortress Press, 1983). A careful New Testament scholar, Scroggs demands that users of the Bible use biblical materials carefully and without violating the integrity of the texts by taking statements out of context or by assuming that modern meanings apply to ancient times, problems and settings.

69. Scroggs, *The New Testament and Homosexuality.* This is elaborated in much more detail here in a careful, scholarly study. Similarly, his analysis of the same prohibition in Romans 1:18–32 supports the point summarized in this paragraph.

70. Scroggs, *The New Testament and Homosexuality.* This discussion is based on both a careful scholarly analysis and a warm investment in the message of the New Testament. He vehemently opposes any distortion of the Bible text or message to fit modern concerns, and seems to find pederasty repulsive, while he tries to treat adult homosexuality as fair-mindedly as he can, although I think he is personally repelled.

71. J. L. Marx, "Sexual Responses Are—Almost—All in the Brain." *Science* 241 (1988): 903–4. Summarizes a symposium entitled "Neuroendocrine Modulation of Central Nervous System Function," held in Galveston, TX in May 1988.

72. This surmise was expressed to suggest to her that human relationships were meaningful and followed comprehensible patterns, and that her husband's behavior was less a reaction to her worth than to motives largely within himself.

73. G. M. Lamsa, *Idioms in the Bible Explained and A Key to the Original Gospels* (New York: Harper & Row, 1985). Lamsa argues that Mark and Luke were derived from Matthew and that careful study of the Aramic originals (to the extent that the texts are reliable) indicates that Jesus was probably forbidding men to marry women who had been dismissed by their former husbands without a formal divorce. The argument is very interesting. Nevertheless, there is a long tradition to the contrary in some denominations that may be very powerful.

74. Abdul-Rauf, *The Islamic View of Women and the Family.*

75. This is permitted by the Qur'an, but not apparently encouraged.

76. Tigers tend to have a hunting range. Males and females unite to mate but then go back to their own hunting ranges. Lions mate for life and the female does the hunting. If she

is unable to hunt, she is unlikely to be accepted by a male as a mate.

77. Pomeroy, *Goddesses, Whores, Wives and Slaves.* This is a careful sifting of the available data by a knowledgeable scholar.

78. The Talmud is a codification of Jewish law, legal decisions, and many other matters that developed over close to a thousand years. It is thirty-five hefty volumes in the Soncino English translation.

79. E. A. Speiser, *Genesis,* 3rd ed., *The Anchor Bible* (Garden City, NY: Doubleday & Co., 1982).

80. Abdul-Rauf, *The Islamic View of Women and the Family.* Some sections are quite lyrical on the value of marriage, sexuality within marriage, the husband's duty to assure a wife's satisfaction, and so on. He deals with women's oppression in some Muslim countries, but somewhat gently.

81. These are statements, comments, and advice of Muhammad, recorded by his companions, that are of nearly the same stature as the Qur'an.

82. K. Cragg and M. Speight, *Islam from Within: Anthology of a Religion* (Belmont, CA: Wadsworth Publishing Co., 1980).

83. There are other exceptions with women as powerful, independent preachers and leaders, such as Aimee Semple McPherson in the early part of this century, and several women who took the lead in pursuing rabbinic training and ordination in the Reform and Conservative movement.

84. Since many Jewish religious practices are observed in the home, the wife's role is very important. Jewish descent is traced through the mother, not the father. Most Jewish women of my acquaintance are formidable.

85. The Catholic bishops, as a group, have not supported ordination for women, but have supported women as deacons, which can be a step toward ordination.

86. The pain of birth and difficulty of farming was intensified, not imposed for the first time, and this was clearly meant as a punishment. Even conservative but careful commentaries recognize this, as in J. H. Hertz, *The Pentateuch and Haftorahs* (London: Soncino Press, 1972), 12. To be cursed was another matter entirely, involving a basic rejection. It seems equivalent to the idea in English law of being declared "outlaw"; that is, outside the protection of the law. A similar idea is expressed

when, after Cain murdered Abel, God put a sign on him to indicate that he was still protected.

87. P. Rieff, *Freud: The Mind of the Moralist* (New York: Viking, 1959).

H. Küng, *Freud and the Problem of God* (New Haven: Yale University Press, 1979).

88. H. Küng, *On Being a Christian* (Garden City: NY, 1976).

89. *The New English Bible with the Apocrypha* (Oxford and Cambridge, England: Oxford University Press and Cambridge University Press, 1970), 83.

90. Leviticus 4 deals with this explicitly.

91. The "h" is strongly aspirated.

92. Lovinger, *Religious Issues in Therapy.* I think that the concept of venial and mortal sins parallels, and may originate from, the distinction between unintentional and avoidable sin.

93. Lamsa, *Idioms in the Bible,* 53. Lamsa grew up in an Aramaic-speaking community that had preserved the ancient language, idioms, customs, and traditions, and argues effectively that there are many misinterpretations and mistranslations of the Bible because of a failure to recognize or to understand idiomatic usage in the original Aramaic language in which Jesus spoke. Lamsa's concise but intriguing book deals with many of these idioms, using the entire Bible.

94. Lovinger, *Religious Issues in Therapy.* See discussion on p. 240, which is based on J. A. T. Robinson, *Can We Trust the New Testament* (Grand Rapids: Eerdmans, 1977).

Chapter 4: Special Challenges of Religious Expression

1. T. Robbins, *Cults, Converts and Charisma: The Sociology of New Religious Movements* (London: Sage Publications, 1988).

2. D. G. Bromley and A. D. Shupe, Jr., *Strange Gods: The Great American Cult Scare* (Boston: Beacon Press, 1981), 12.

3. J. B. Judis, "Rev. Moon's Rising Political Influence," *U. S. News & World Report* (Mar. 27, 1989).

4. R. J. Lovinger, "Religion in the Stabilization and Regulation of the Self." (Paper delivered at the American Psychological Association Convention, New Orleans, LA, 1989).

5. Both Bromley and Shupe, and Robbins, in their separate

reviews agree on the difficulty, expense and relative ineffectiveness of "brainwashing."

6. J. B. Judis, "Rev. Moon's Rising Political Influence."

7. A good example is to be found on the television program "*48 Hours*" broadcast over CBS on June 15, 1989.

8. Bromley and Shupe, *Strange Gods,* 204.

9. T. Robbins, *Cults, Converts and Charisma.*

10. Bromley and Shupe, *Strange Gods.*

11. See Note 7.

12. Bromley and Shupe, *Strange Gods,* 91.

13. Bromley and Shupe, *Strange Gods.*

14. R. S. Ellwood, "Occult Movements in America," *Encyclopedia of the American Religious Experience.* ed. C. H. Lippy and P. W. Williams (New York: Charles Scribner's Sons, 1988), 711–22.

15. A. Lyons, *Satan Wants You: The Cult of Devil Worship in America* (New York: The Mysterious Press, 1988).

16. Lyons, *Satan Wants You,* 9.

17. R. S. Ellwood, "Occult Movements in America," *Encyclopedia of the American Religious Experience* ed. Lippy and Williams, 721.

18. Lyons, *Satan Wants You.*

19. B. Magid, "The Evil Self," *Dynamic Psychotherapy* 6 (1988):99–113.

20. J. Jaynes, *The Origins of Consciousness in the Breakdown of the Bicameral Mind* (Boston: Houghton-Miflin, 1976).

21. This is represented in numerous ways in the Bible. "God said . . . ," and Adam names the animals in Genesis, or "In the beginning was the Word" (John 1:1, *The Anchor Bible*).

22. See chapter 3, note 44.

23. H. S. Kushner, *When Bad Things Happen to Good People* (New York: Avon Books, 1981), 37.

24. D. Bakan, *Disease, Pain & Sacrifice: Toward a Psychology of Suffering* (Boston: Beacon Press, 1971).

25. Here I think Bakan implicitly distinguished between *pain,* which is more rooted in sensory structures, and *suffering,* which has a larger mental component and implies *enduring* and, in older usage, *allowing.*

26. H. Selye's famous work *The Stress of Life* (New York:

McGraw-Hill, 1956) is a popular summary of his work on "protective" reactions to stress and the problems such defensive reactions give rise to.

27. Arising from Freud's original ideas. See also A. Freud, *The Ego and the Mechanisms of Defense* (New York: International Universities Press, 1946).

28. D. Bakan, *Disease, Pain & Sacrifice,* 126.

29. In Judaism this is called *Kiddush haShem* or Sanctification of the Name. In Christianity, the word derives from the Greek *martus* meaning witness.

30. Adapted from D. L. Rosenhan and M. E. P. Seligman, *Abnormal Psychology* (New York: Norton, 1984), 350.

31. B. P. Karon and G. VandenBos, *Psychotherapy of Schizophrenia: The Treatment of Choice* (New York: Jason Aronson, 1981).

32. I am indebted to Gerald B. Fuller for this pithy statement.

Chapter 5: Counseling, Collaboration, and Referral

1. There are some very conservative Protestant denominations that claim that Catholics are not Christian.

2. An example of the negative effects of insufficient candor is reported in: R. J. Lovinger, "Religious Issues in the Psychotherapy of a Borderline Patient," in *Psychotherapy of the Religious Patient* ed. M. H. Spero (Springfield, IL: C. C. Thomas, 1985), 181–207.

3. E. P. Cohen, "An Exploratory Study of Religiously Committed, Psychoanalytically Oriented Clinicians" (Unpublished doctoral dissertation, City University of New York, 1986).

4. S. S. Tomkins, *Affect, Imagery, Consciousness,* vol. 1 (New York: Springer Publishing Co., 1962).

5. C. R. Rogers, *Client-Centered Therapy* (Boston: Houghton-Miflin, 1951). Rogers is a foremost and persuasive exemplar of this view. What he rightly criticized was diagnosis without concern for the client.

6. P. W. Pruyser, "Assessment of the Patient's Religious Attitudes in the Psychiatric Case Study," *Bulletin of the Menninger Clinic* 35 (1971):272–91.

———, "The Seamy Side of Current Religious Beliefs," *Bulletin of the Menninger Clinic* 41 (1977):329–48.

J. L. Rubins, "Neurotic Attitudes Toward Religion," *American Journal of Psychoanalysis* 15 (1955):71–81.

L. Salzman, "The Psychology of Religious and Ideological Conversion," *Psychiatry* 16 (1953):177–87.

7. See note 6.

8. F. A. Coyle, Jr. and P. Erdberg, "A Liberalizing Approach to Maladaptive Fundamentalist Hyperreligiosity," *Psychotherapy: Therapy, Research and Practice* 6 (1969):140–42.

9. R. Young, *Young's Analytical Concordance to the Bible* (Grand Rapids: Eerdmans, 1970).

10. A. Jones, ed. *The Jerusalem Bible* (Garden City, NY: Doubleday & Co., 1966). This version was translated under Roman Catholic auspices. *New English Bible* (Oxford: Oxford University Press, 1970). This was translated under English Protestant sponsorship.

11. S. Forward, *Toxic Parents: Overcoming Their Hurtful Legacy and Reclaiming Your Life* (New York: Bantam Books, 1989).

12. M. G. Weiss and T. Woodman, "The Practical Use of Forgiveness in Counseling." (Paper delivered at the Ninety-fourth American Psychological Association Convention, August, 1986).

13. General sources for counselor and client include:

Robert Alter, *The Art of Biblical Narrative* (New York: Basic Books, 1981).

Isaac Asimov, *Asimov's Guide to the Bible: The Old Testament* (New York: Avon Books, 1968).

Isaac Asimov, *Asimov's Guide to the Bible: The New Testament* (New York: Avon Books, 1969).

Charles H. Lippy and Peter W. Williams, eds., *Encyclopedia of the American Religious Experience* (New York: Charles Scribner's Sons, 1988).

Gabriel Josipovici, *The Book of God: A Response to the Bible* (New Haven: Yale University Press, 1988).

George M. Lamsa, *Idioms in the Bible Explained and A Key to the Original Gospels* (New York: Harper & Row, 1985).

Paul W. Pruyser, *Between Belief and Unbelief* (New York: Harper & Row, 1974).

David Stacey, *Interpreting the Bible* (New York: Hawthorn Books, 1977).

Further information on Love, Marriage, and Sexuality may be found in:

W. G. Cole, *Sex and Love in the Bible* (New York: Association Press, 1959).

A. Kosnik, W. Carroll, A. Cunningham, R. Modias, and J. Schulte, *Human Sexuality: New Directions in American Catholic Thought* (Mahwah, NJ: Paulist Press, 1977).

Rafael Patai, *Family, Love and the Bible* (London: MacGibbon and Kee, 1960).

There are a number of bible translations with more or less extensive explanatory notes. The most thorough, scholarly and objective is the Anchor Bible series, but the Jerusalem Bible is highly regarded by many Catholics and has recently been issued in a new translation as the New Jerusalem Bible. The New English Bible has wide respect among many Protestants but it has not been highly regarded for its literary qualities by some commentators. The recent translations, with commentaries by the Jewish Publication Society are also well regarded by many Jews.

14. A. Compaan, "Consultation and Referral Development With Evangelical Clergy." (Paper delivered at the Ninety-second American Psychological Association Convention, 1984).

15. J. W. Baldwin, Jr., "Counseling and Consulting Patterns Among Evangelical Protestant Clergy." (Paper delivered at the Ninety-second American Psychological Association Convention, 1984).

16. A. Compaan, "Consultation and Referral Development."

17. "Pleasure" is used here in the sense of appropriate satisfaction, not indiscriminate or destructive sensation seeking.

18. A. Compaan, "Consultation and Referral Development."

19. Rabbi comes from a Hebrew word meaning master, as in schoolmaster. Hence the function of the rabbi was as a teacher, judge, legal expert but not as a preacher, although he or she has that role in this country.

20. When I was in the Army, shortly after the Korean war ended, the Jewish chaplain on the base was an electrical engineer, work which he expected to continue to do when he returned to civilian life. However, when he was to be drafted, he chose to be a second lieutenant in the Chaplain Corps rather than a private in the Engineers Corps.

21. P. W. Schubert, "Religion in Clinical Practice," *Newsletter Division 36—American Psychological Association* 11 (1986):4–5.

22. C. M. Ideran, "Assessment and Psychotherapy With Conservative Seminarians." (Paper delivered at the Ninety-fourth American Psychological Association Convention, 1986).

23. The children of ministers are often under extra pressure to set a good example, not embarrass the parent, excel in one or more areas, be active in church youth groups, etc. This leads to the problem of being a "p. k." or "preacher's kid."

24. D. L. Araoz, "Marital Therapy With Former Priests," *Psychotherapy, Theory, Research and Practice* 9 (1972):337–39.

25. D. L. Araoz, "Marital Therapy With Former Priests."

26. E. P. Cohen, "Exploratory Study of Clinicians."

27. S. P. Chesner and R. F. Baumeister, "Effect of Therapist's Disclosure of Religious Beliefs on the Intimacy of Client Self-Disclosure," *Journal of Social and Clinical Psychology* 3 (1985):97–105.

28. In the Chesner and Baumeister study, the "therapist" (it was an experimental simulation of a therapy situation) wore an obvious religious symbol.

Chapter 6: Approaches to the Bible in Counseling

1. This word originated from the name of the Phoenician port *Bublos* from which papyrus was exported to Greece. From W. Morris, ed., *The Heritage Illustrated Dictionary of the English Language* (Boston: Houghton-Mifflin, 1979), 129. However, the Greek seems to have been *ta biblia* or "the little books" reflecting its diverse nature. See N. Frye, *The Great Code: The Bible and Literature* (New York: Harcourt Brace Jovanovich, 1981).

2. H. Smith, *The Religions of Man* (New York: Harper & Row, 1965).

3. H. Smith, *The Religions of Man.*

4. The expansion of Islam has tended to bring the Qur'an along in its original language because of the intimate link between Arabic poetry and the Qur'an. Frye, *The Great Code.*

5. The Sunna contains, among other things a collection of Muhammad's statements, used for guidance. The name of the majority group within Islam, the Sunni, is derived from this.

6. See chapter 1 for more detail under *A Brief Historical Survey.*

7. E. Fackenheim, *God's Presence in History* (New York: Harper & Row, 1970).

8. From "seventy" in Greek, for a legend that it was separately translated in identical fashion by 72 scholars.

9. This version of Greek, *koine,* was once thought to be a sacred form of the language but was later found to be the everyday language of the people.

10. G. Josipovici, *The Book of God: A Response to the Bible* (New Haven: Yale University Press, 1988). This is one of a number of examples that Josipovici's thoughtful discussion illuminates. His extended but very readable discussion of the problems of translation is a useful treatment that can be of help with a client who has an issue about a particular translated version of the Bible.

11. D. Daiches, "Translating the Bible," *Commentary* (May, 1970), 59–68.

12. R. E. Friedman, *Who Wrote the Bible?* (New York: Perennial Library, 1989).

13. Much of the Bible conforms to the standards of oral storytelling which gives it its special linguistic qualities. N. Frye, *The Great Code.*

14. See chapter 1, note 6 and chapter 3, page 98.

15. R. Alter, *The Art of Biblical Narrative* (New York: Basic Books, 1981). Alter's analysis of the literary art of the Bible contributes much to an appreciative reading of the Old Testament.

16. Alter, *The Art of Biblical Narrative.*

17. Alter, *The Art of Biblical Narrative,* 126.

18. Good, non-technical aids to more easily understand biblical materials are given in chapter 5, note 13.

19. G. M. Lamsa, *Idioms in the Bible Explained and A Key to the Original Gospels* (New York: Harper & Row, 1985).

20. G. Josipovici, *The Book of God.*

21. G. Josipovici, *The Book of God,* 225–29.

22. I got this from Hans Küng in his *On Being a Christian.*

23. St. Paul, in Ephesians 5:21–29 gives a famous recommendation that is often taken as "women, submit to your husbands," yet this is rendered differently in different translations. Four

such translations are compared side by side in R. J. Lovinger, *Working With Religious Issues in Therapy.* (New York: Jason Aronson, 1984), 228–29.

24. G. Josipovici, *The Book of God.*

25. Literary criticism means the attempt to understand the meanings, forms, structures, and such of any piece of writing. It is not primarily a criticism of the worth of the writing. When applied to the Bible, such literary analyses attempt to grasp the meanings, structure, and coherences of the text. There are several recent and available books that can help interested but non-technical readers given in chapter 5, note 12.

THE CONTINUUM COUNSELING LIBRARY
Books of Related Interest

———Denyse Beaudet
ENCOUNTERING THE MONSTER
Pathways in Children's Dreams
Based on original empirical research, and with recourse to the works of Jung, Neumann, Eliade, Marie-Louise Franz, and others, this book offers proven methods of approaching and understanding the dream life of children. $17.95

———Robert W. Buckingham
CARE OF THE DYING CHILD
A Practical Guide for Those Who Help Others
"Buckingham's book delivers a powerful, poignant message deserving a wide readership."—*Library Journal* $17.95

———Alastair V. Campbell, ed.
A DICTIONARY OF PASTORAL CARE
Provides information on the essentials of counseling and the kinds of problems encountered in pastoral practice. The approach is interdenominational and interdisciplinary. Contains over 300 entries by 185 authors in the fields of theology, philosophy, psychology, and sociology as well as from the theoretical background of psychotherapy and counseling. $24.50

———David A. Crenshaw
BEREAVEMENT
Counseling the Grieving throughout the Life Cycle
Grief is examined from a life cycle perspective, infancy to old age. Special losses and practical strategies for frontline caregivers highlight this comprehensive guidebook. $17.95

———H. J. Eysenck, W. Arnold, and R. Meili, eds.
ENCYCLOPEDIA OF PSYCHOLOGY
Covering all aspects of psychology, this book features brief definitions and essays by subject specialists.
"An authoritative reference book in a clear and intelligible language. Essential."—*Booklist* $60.00

———Reuben Fine
THE HISTORY OF PSYCHOANALYSIS
New Expanded Edition
"Objective, comprehensive, and readable. A rare work. Highly recommended, whether as an introduction to the field or as a fresh overview to those already familiar with it."—*Contemporary Psychology* $24.95 paperback

———Lucy Freeman
FIGHT AGAINST FEARS
With a new Introduction by
Flora Rheta Schreiber
More than a million copies sold; the new—and only available—edition of the first, and still best, true story of a modern woman's journey of self-discovery through psychoanalysis. $10.95

———Lucy Freeman
OUR INNER WORLD OF RAGE
Understanding and Transforming the Power of Anger
A psychoanalytic examination of the anger that burns within us and which can be used to save or slowly destroy us. Sheds light on all expressions of rage, from the murderer to the suicide to those of us who feel depressed and angry but are unaware of the real cause. $15.95

———Lucy Freeman and Kerstin Kupfermann
THE POWER OF FANTASY
Where Our Daydreams Come From, and How They Can Help or Harm Us
This is the first book to explain the role of both daydreams and unconscious fantasies in our lives, helping us to distinguish between those that can unleash our creativity and those that can emotionally cripple us. $16.95

———John Gerdtz and Joel Bregman, M. D.
AUTISM
A Practical Guide for Those Who Help Others
An up-to-date and comprehensive guidebook for everyone who works with autistic children, adolescents, adults, and their families. Includes latest information on medications. $17.95

———Marion Howard
HOW TO HELP YOUR TEENAGER POSTPONE SEXUAL INVOLVEMENT
Based on a national educational program that works, this book advises parents, teachers, and counselors on how they can help their teens resist social and peer pressures regarding sex. $14.95

———Marion Howard
SOMETIMES I WONDER ABOUT ME
Teenagers and Mental Health
Combines fictional narratives with sound, understandable professional advice to help teenagers recognize the difference between serious problems and normal problems of adjustment. $9.95

———E. Clay Jorgensen
CHILD ABUSE
A Practical Guide for Those Who Help Others
Essential information and practical advice for caregivers called upon to help both child and parent in child abuse. $16.95

———Eugene Kennedy
CRISIS COUNSELING
The Essential Guide for Nonprofessional Counselors
"An outstanding author of books on personal growth selects types of personal crises that our present life style has made commonplace and suggests effective ways to deal with them."—*Best Sellers* $11.95

———Eugene Kennedy and Sara Charles, M. D.
ON BECOMING A COUNSELOR
A Basic Guide for Nonprofessional Counselors
New expanded edition of an indispensable resource. A patient-oriented, clinically directed field guide to understanding and responding to troubled people. $27.95 hardcover $15.95 paperback

———Eugene Kennedy
SEXUAL COUNSELING
A Practical Guide for Those Who Help Others
Newly revised and up-to-date edition, with a new chapter on [the counselor and] AIDS, of an essential book on counseling people with sexual problems. $17.95

———Bonnie Lester
WOMEN AND AIDS
A Practical Guide for Those Who Help Others
Provides positive ways for women to deal with their fears, and to help others who react with fear to people who have AIDS. $15.95

———Robert J. Lovinger
RELIGION AND COUNSELING
The Psychological Impact of Religious Belief
How counselors and clergy can best understand the important emotional significance of religious thoughts and feelings. $17.95

———Helen B. McDonald and Audrey I. Steinhorn
HOMOSEXUALITY
A Practical Guide to Counseling Gays, Lesbians, and Their Families
A sensitive guide to better understanding and counseling gays, lesbians, and their parents, at every stage of their lives. $16.95

———Janice N. McLean and Sheila A. Knights
PHOBICS AND OTHER PANIC VICTIMS
A Practical Guide for Those Who Help Them
"A must for the phobic, spouse and family, and for the physician and support people who help them. It can spell the difference between partial therapy with partial results and comprehensive therapy and recovery."—Arthur B. Hardy, M. D., Founder, TERRAP Phobia Program, and Past President, Phobia Society of America $17.95

———John B. Mordock and William Van Ornum
CRISIS COUNSELING WITH CHILDREN AND ADOLESCENTS
A Guide for Nonprofessional Counselors
New Expanded Edition
"Every parent should keep this book on the shelf right next to the nutrition, medical, and Dr. Spock books."—*Marriage & Family Living* $12.95

———Cherry Boone O'Neill
DEAR CHERRY
Questions and Answers on Eating Disorders
Practical and inspiring advice on eating disorders from the best-selling author of *Starving for Attention* $8.95

———Paul G. Quinnett
ON BECOMING A HEALTH AND HUMAN SERVICES MANAGER
A Practical Guide for Clinicians and Counselors
A new and essential guide to management for everyone in the helping professions—from mental health to nursing, from social work to teaching. $19.95

———Paul G. Quinnett
SUICIDE: THE FOREVER DECISION
For Those Thinking About Suicide,
and For Those Who Know, Love, or Counsel Them
"A treasure—this book can help save lives. It will be especially valuable not only to those who are thinking about suicide but to such nonprofessional counselors as teachers, clergy, doctors, nurses, and to experienced therapists."—William Van Ornum, psychotherapist and author $18.95 hardcover $8.95 paperback

———Judah L. Ronch
ALZHEIMER'S DISEASE
A Practical Guide for Those Who Help Others
Must reading for everyone—from family members to professional caregivers—who must deal with the effects of this tragic disease on a daily basis. Filled with illustrative examples as well as facts, this book provides sensitive insights into dealing with one's feelings as well as with such practical advice as how to choose long-term care. $17.95

———Theodore Isaac Rubin, M. D.
ANTI-SEMITISM: A DISEASE OF THE MIND
"A most poignant and lucid psychological examination of a severe emotional disease. Dr. Rubin offers hope and understanding to the victim and to the bigot. A splendid job!"—Dr. Herbert S. Strean $14.95

———John R. Shack
COUPLES COUNSELING
A Practical Guide for Those Who Help Others
An essential guide to dealing with the 20 percent of all counseling situations that involve the relationship of two people. $17.95

———Stuart Sutherland
THE INTERNATIONAL DICTIONARY OF PSYCHOLOGY
This new dictionary of psychology also covers a wide range of related disciplines, from anthropology to sociology. $49.95

———Joan Leslie Taylor
IN THE LIGHT OF DYING
The Journals of a Hospice Volunteer
A rare and beautiful book about death and dying that affirms life and will inspire an attitude of love. "Beautifully recounts the healing (our own) that results from service to others, and might well be considered as required reading for hospice volunteers."—Stephen Levine $17.95

———Montague Ullman, M. D. and Claire Limmer, M. S., eds.
THE VARIETY OF DREAM EXPERIENCE
Expanding Our Ways of Working With Dreams
"Lucidly describes the beneficial impact dream analysis can have in diverse fields and in society as a whole. An erudite, illuminating investigation."—*Booklist* $19.95 hardcover $14.95 paperback

———William Van Ornum and Mary W. Van Ornum
TALKING TO CHILDREN ABOUT NUCLEAR WAR
"A wise book. A needed book. An urgent book."—Dr. Karl A. Menninger $15.95 hardcover $7.95 paperback

———Kathleen Zraly and David Swift, M. D.
ANOREXIA, BULIMIA, AND COMPULSIVE OVEREATING
A Practical Guide for Counselors and Families
A psychiatrist and an eating disorders specialist provide new and helpful approaches for everyone who knows, loves, or counsels victims of anorexia, bulimia, and chronic overeating. $17.95

At your bookstore, or to order directly, send your check or money order (adding $2.00 extra per book for postage and handling, up to $6.00 maximum) to: The Continuum Publishing Company, 370 Lexington Avenue, New York, NY, 10017. Prices are subject to change.